FINE GOLD FROM YORKSHIRE

Faith Cook

ƏP

EP BOOKS

1st Floor Venture House, 6 Silver Court, Watchmead, Welwyn Garden City, UK, AL7 1TS

http://www.epbooks.org

admin@epbooks.org

EP Books are distributed in the USA by:

JPL Distribution

3741 Linden Avenue Southeast

Grand Rapids, MI 49548

orders@jplbooks.com

British Library Cataloguing in Publication Data available

ISBN 978-1-78397-194-7

Printed and bound in Great Britain by Bell and Bain Ltd, Glasgow

Contents

Foreword

Perhaps you have to be born in Yorkshire to realise how much this county means to us, and how bewildering it is when others don't quite understand our love of all things Yorkshire.

We know we are a county of characters, but we don't mind that. We are characterised by grit. We don't even mind people smirking at us. We're proud of Yorkshire sports people, entertainers, artists, scientists, inventors, writers and even some politicians, though probably our most famous political activist was Guy Fawkes! We love the fact that we chat with those whom we sit next to on a bus, meet at a local 'chippy', on a train, in a coffee shop, or standing in a queue.

We are famed for our Yorkshire Pudding, fish and chips, Yorkshire Parkin, Wensleydale cheese, rhubarb and liquorice, as well as Rowntree's chocolate and Yorkshire Tea. We have more dry stone walling than any other place in the UK (thousands of miles of it) and England's longest waterfall. And who doesn't love the Yorkshire terrier? The spring-loaded mousetrap, the hansom cab, cat's eyes, the kilner jar, the glider-type aircraft, the Bailey bridge, the crow's nest and Sheffield steel were all invented by Yorkshiremen. Marks and Spencer didn't start in just any county, but in Yorkshire!

We have our Dales (thirty-eight of them), the Three Peaks, the Moors and coastline, with its twelve lighthouses. Our cathedrals (eight of them) and abbeys (ten of them, Whitby's dating back to

657AD) enrich the county. It's not too long ago that our skylines had dark symbols of the coal mines underneath (there were fifty in Yorkshire). We are known for our wool and textile industry, and our blunt speaking. We have produced two of the UK's most well-known furniture makers—Thomas Chippendale of Otley and Robert Thompson of Kilburn, 'the Mouseman'—and are known for our wool and textile industries.

Famous for its cricket, Yorkshire was home to some of the all-time greats. Herbert Sutcliffe (who scored 38,558 runs in his career), Freddy Trueman, George Hirst and Geoffrey Boycott. Len Hutton said, 'In an England cricket eleven, the flesh may be of the South, but the bone is of the North, and the backbone is Yorkshire.' Lord's Cricket Ground in London was founded by Thomas Lord who was born in Thirsk. As well, Yorkshire is the birthplace of both rugby league and quoits. Olympians Alistair and Jonny Brownlee of Horsforth have made the triathlon look a walkover!

But for me, the most interesting aspect of Yorkshire is its great Christian heritage. There are Christians from the county who have taken the gospel to the furthest corners of the world, whilst others have worked and ministered nearer to home. They have left an indelible impact on history and society. Faith Cook, biographer par excellence, has presented us with a magnificent smörgåsbord of the lives of some of history's most well-known Yorkshire Christians. Of course, there are numerous unsung heroes who also experienced the transforming power of God to forgive them, change them and use them to be of benefit to others through their talents and service. But it is this transformation that brings together such a variety of characters. Their abilities are very different, but their common faith in Jesus is the thread which unites them. They are remembered in history books by their achievements, but to really understand each of them, one has to look beyond their works to their trust in Jesus Christ. Each came to the definite point in their lives when they turned from their own ways and submitted to the Lordship of Christ. They each believed that when Jesus was crucified, he was taking on himself their sin, so that he was dying in their place, paying the price of their wrong. They trusted the risen, living Jesus to forgive them and take over their lives as they became his followers. Each of them had a Christian conversion.

Sadly, today in Yorkshire there are comparatively few who follow Christ. Whereas once it seemed that every estate and village had its chapel and church, today they have closed and Jesus has been marginalised by many. Most would probably agree that everyone is guilty of sinning against God in one way or another. But the Christian believes that all wrong is serious. It is only through Jesus who loves us, died for us, rose again and commands that we should turn from our self-centred, godless living that we may receive the new life which he freely offers. As one enters into a relationship with God, he makes all things new. This book is testimony to that. And the God who did amazing things in history is still at work in lives today.

Roger Carswell

1. Titus Salt of Saltaire: a lasting legacy

A tall young man, dark haired and with a fresh-looking face, was walking slowly through downtown Liverpool. With quick sharp eyes he was taking in all he saw as he passed to left and right. Titus Salt, in business with his father Daniel Salt, was a wool-stapler—a term now fallen into disuse. Essentially his task was to buy raw wool from the producers, sort and grade it and then sell it on to the manufacturers to be woven into a wide variety of woollen items. Described as 'every inch a man', Titus missed little as he walked through Liverpool that day. And as he passed a rundown looking warehouse of a firm of Liverpool brokers on the docks he noticed a number of dirty looking bales stacked out in the open. One or two were torn in places and some type of wool bulged out. Wool? This might be a new sort that he and his father could use in their business, Daniel Salt and Son, Wool-staplers of Bradford. Approaching the bales Titus pulled a few strands from one tear in the sacking and twisted it between his fingers, testing the length of the fibres. He decided to take it home to experiment further.

Titus Salt had a burning ambition to succeed. He was what we today would call an entrepreneur—one who was willing to venture, take risks, experiment and refuse to give in. Born in 1803 in Morley, West Yorkshire, then a village of little more than two thousand, Titus was the oldest of a family of seven, although two had died in infancy. Morley was a place that John Wesley frequently visited on his travels up and down the country, and here religious convictions ran deep. His parents, Daniel and Grace Salt, were Bible loving people and from early days Grace taught her young son to cherish the Bible, to pray and to serve and follow God. A well-worn Bible, given to him by his mother, accompanied him throughout life, the inscription on the fly leaf read:

> May this blest volume ever lie
> Close to thy heart and near thine eye;
> Till life's last hour thy soul engage,
> And be thy chosen heritage.

Although Titus Salt was interested in the wool he had seen in Liverpool, he was wary. Once before he had experimented with a new type of wool and the firm had hovered on the brink of disaster as a result. Donskoi wool, a product of sheep from Russia was a coarse and somewhat tangled fibre and not obviously well adapted for the fine fabrics in demand particularly in the worsted industry. Titus had bought a large quantity and tried to sell it to the manufacturers, but no one would take the risk of buying it from him.

As a result, the days were bleak for the firm, but Titus was not one to give in easily. He still thought there was potential in Donskoi wool. If he could not sell it, he decided, he would spin it into yarn and weave it himself. So he bought a disused mill, fitted it up with the necessary machinery and began the process of weaving the Donskoi wool. To the astonishment of all the other manufacturers, it turned into the most beautiful fabric. This single product shot the ailing Daniel Salt firm to success. Soon two more Bradford mills were purchased to cope with the increasing demand.

Now in a better financial position Titus also had other matters in mind besides buying wool. On a business trip to Grimsby he had found time to pay a visit to a farmer with a numerous family. Rumour had it that among his children were some very beautiful daughters. Although naturally shy and retiring by disposition, Titus was determined to meet these girls; he had heard of one in particular whose praises were being passed around. But on reaching the farm he spotted another daughter, the youngest of the girls, sixteen-year-old Caroline. He was struck at first sight, and despite the age difference between them for he was twenty-five, he determined that this was the girl he wanted to marry. But Titus was not impulsive and he waited until Caroline was eighteen before they married. Clearly he had found something much more precious than wool to bring home that day. And a happy boisterous home they built as eleven children were born to the couple, though some died in infancy as so often happened in those days.

It was at this point in his life that Titus Salt first came across the new wool in Liverpool. As he experimented with the specimen he had taken home he realised that it might well have real potential. Returning to Liverpool he plucked up courage to make further enquiries.

'Yes, the bales of wool are still for sale,' he was told. 'It is Alpaca wool from an animal resembling a small llama called a paca or alpaca that grazes on the mountain slopes of Peru. In fact, we are about to send the whole consignment back to Peru because no-one here wants it.'

Expressing his interest, Titus now took a larger sample home, carefully washing the material. He then combed the uneven hairs, tested the length and strength of the strands. With further trials, he was now sure of the potential of this new wool. It had turned out to be soft and silky yet warm and resilient and would make some of the fine dresses so popular with ladies. But his father still remembered the early misfortune with the Donskoi wool and strongly recommended that Titus leave Alpaca wool alone. 'Have nothing to do with the nasty stuff,' a friend warned. But the young man was insistent. Returning to Liverpool once more he entered the dingy warehouse and to the astonishment of the merchants offered to buy all three hundred bales of the wool for eight pence a pound in weight. Was the man mad, they wondered. But Titus was seldom saner.

Many difficulties had yet to be overcome, however. This Alpaca wool would need specialised machinery to card, spin and weave it into the beautiful material that Titus had found it could become. Undeterred, he set about having the machinery built, but they were anxious days. What if he was wrong? But at last an amazing product began to take shape before his eyes. So began the most astonishing rise of Daniel Salt and Son until Titus was the largest employer in Bradford with five mills in operation.

If this were the end of the Titus Salt story, we should conclude that here was an exceptional Yorkshire man with a head for business—a great employer and a man of faith. But there is more to the story, much more. He was also deeply concerned for the welfare of his employees and their children. Numbering well over two thousand, many lived in appalling conditions. Pollution was rife in Bradford, the atmosphere foul, houses crammed together with sanitation virtually non-existent. Consequently, life expectancy was little over eighteen years with many of Salt's finest young workers dying at an early age.

Living in a beautiful home himself, a mansion known as Crow Nest some miles outside the city, Titus knew that something radical must be done to alleviate the horrifying conditions of his workers. Between 1848 and 1849 he had held the position of Chief Constable of Bradford and was the second to be appointed as mayor of the city. Surely, he thought, he had a duty to do something. Added to this his mills were scattered throughout Bradford, adding to the pollution and making communications between them difficult. There was only one solution. He must move his entire workforce to a more healthy environment.

After careful searching, Titus Salt found the ideal place—a few miles north of Bradford not far from Shipley lay an idyllic area on the edge of the moors and nestling under the Pennine range. The River Aire ran along the valley and the Leeds-Liverpool canal had been built nearby, plus a railway line which would facilitate transporting goods. The atmosphere was sweet and clean with the abundant supply of water necessary for the processing of the Alpaca wool.

Work began immediately to construct a mill of gigantic proportions for the day. Built of yellow sandstone, it has been described as the largest industrial mill in the world. At last in 1853 work was complete. A huge opening banquet was laid on to coincide with Titus Salt's own fiftieth birthday. Held in the combing shed of the new building, it catered for over 3000 guests, of whom as many as 2,500 were his own workforce. The food was magnificent: sides of beef, lamb, ham, roast duck, partridges, grouse and even pigeons. Desserts followed and all replete with 4,200 glasses of wine and 750 of champagne, even though Titus himself was a teetotaller.

And all this was only a beginning. Titus Salt's next task was to build attractive stone houses for his workers, an astonishing contrast to the slum hovels from which they had come. Before long he had completed over eight hundred homes and as the years passed, facilities of all sorts were added including a Congregational church, a hospital, a school, a library, a recreation ground, a park and boathouse with more besides. Appropriately enough the new village was called Saltaire, to combine the name of its founder with the name of the river that flowed nearby. One item not provided for the residents of Saltaire was a licensed premise for the sale of alcohol. Titus had known what ruin was caused in many homes in the rundown streets of Bradford through alcohol. When one public house, now a restaurant, did finally open after Titus's death it was named in mock humour 'Don't tell Titus'.

With so much outwardly to commend him, it may come as a surprise that this philanthropic and upright man, who had also supported his church with astonishing generosity, suffered from a lack of spiritual assurance of his own personal salvation for much of his life. Although taught from childhood to revere the Scriptures and honour God, it was not until his declining years that Titus appeared to gain a new and liberating dimension in his own relationship to the Lord Jesus Christ. We learn this from an early biographer the Rev. R. Balgarnie who was evidently also a personal friend.

Preaching from the words of Christ, *Come to me, all you who are weary and heavy laden and I will give you rest*, Balgarnie tells us of the deep effect that message had on Titus. 'I am one who needs such rest,' Titus had confessed, and then asked a vital question, 'What must I do to be saved?' Balgarnie writes:

> We do not say this anxious inquirer had no difficulties to be overcome, or doubts to be met, or fallacious conceptions of the method of salvation to be removed. Of these he had many, but he was willing to become as a little child, that he might enter the kingdom of Heaven. In short, it was evident that such an earnest seeker after rest and truth would ere long be a happy finder ... Still, the light did not burst upon his mind at once: it came upon him gradually, like the dawn. After this he seemed always ready to be instructed in the Way of Life.

A man of few words, Salt has left us few accounts of his personal faith, or of his convictions and the way he drew courage from God to persevere. All must therefore be gleaned from his way of life. The number of noble causes that Titus Salt chose to support are too many to enumerate. High on his heart was the work of Sunday Schools and the importance of giving the young early instruction in Christian truths. The London City Mission received multiple gifts. Young men wishing to train for Christian ministry were encouraged by his support, and a place of worship built in Bradford itself. Little wonder that Queen Victoria chose to grant this generous-hearted businessman a knighthood, giving him the title of Sir Titus Salt in 1869 when he was sixty-six.

But Sir Titus Salt's health was fast fading. He suffered repeatedly from vicious periods of gout and after each attack he was weaker than before. Walking became ever more difficult and he was seldom seen in public. But if his body was failing, his trust in Christ was secure. Yet he was always a little diffident about the strength of his faith. Near the end, someone asked him if 'his faith in Christ Jesus were firm, his hopes clear, and prospects bright?' His answer was typical. 'No', he replied, 'not so much as I should like them to be; but all my trust is in him. He is the only foundation on which I rest. Nothing else! Nothing else!'

Sir Titus lingered in great weakness until 29 December 1879. His assurance in death was not based on his generosity or of the thousands he had lifted from wretched poverty, but on his Saviour. Among his last words was a simple assurance of Christ's goodness. 'How kind he is to me!' he whispered.

The whole of Bradford seemed to be in mourning when he died. On the day of his funeral, shops were closed, blinds drawn, bells tolled as the hearse was carried slowly through the streets. It is estimated that ten thousand mourners followed the coffin of Bradford's great son and benefactor. After reaching the outskirts of Bradford a different throng followed the hearse as it was borne in an unadorned carriage for the three miles out to Saltaire. Here a simple service was held before burying their hero in the village he had created and among the people he had loved. So passed one of Yorkshire's greatest men and certainly among the most generous.

2. Anne Brontë: Yorkshire's got talent

There must be few Yorkshire men and women who do not feel a sense of personal pride when they hear the word 'Haworth' or read some reference to the achievements of the Brontë sisters. To write anything further on the talents of these three young women is an audacious if not arrogant enterprise. And yet to omit any reference to them in a work dedicated to the lives of some of the best of Yorkshire's sons and daughters would be ignorant, if not remiss.

Of the three it is perhaps Anne Brontë who is least well known. Charlotte Brontë's novel *Jane Eyre* and Emily's *Wuthering Heights* usually take pride of place over Anne's lesser known works: *Agnes Grey* and *The Tenant of Wildfell Hall*. But as we hope to show, Anne's novels are at least equal to those of her sisters if not in some respects superior to them.

Anne was the youngest of Patrick and Maria Brontë's six children: five girls and an only son named Branwell. When Patrick arrived as the new curate in the grey windswept village of Haworth in 1820 Anne was just a few months old. The village had known amazing days seventy years earlier when William Grimshaw was the curate of St Michael's and all Angels. John and Charles Wesley and George Whitefield had each been frequent visiting preachers in those days, with crowds numbering over five thousand flocking to the village on Communion Sundays to worship and listen. John Wesley could say of Grimshaw himself, 'He carries fire with him wherever he goes.' Those heady times had long passed before the Brontës arrived in Haworth but Patrick's preaching followed in the same evangelical tradition as that of his great predecessor.

Tragedy struck the young family when Maria Brontë died of cancer the following year, leaving six motherless children. 'Oh my poor children,' she cried out in anguish again and again when she knew she was dying. Her eldest, Maria, was only seven at the time and Anne little more than eighteen months. Maria Brontë's sister, Elizabeth, who had come to nurse her sister remained in Haworth for the rest of her life and virtually brought up the family.

When Cowan Bridge, a school for clergymen's daughters, opened in 1823 with a list of highly respected patrons, Patrick saw it as the answer to his intractable problem of how to educate his daughters at a price he could afford. Maria, Elizabeth, Charlotte and Emily were all sent to Cowan Bridge, but the grievous deaths of the two older girls with tuberculosis within a few weeks of each other in 1825, is well known. Maria and Elizabeth were just eleven and ten. Fearing for the younger two, Patrick hastily brought Charlotte and Emily home.

For the following few years the Brontë children were largely home educated by Patrick himself, with the help of the children's aunt. Charlotte also took her part with her younger siblings as she grew older. With many books in Patrick's library at their disposal the Brontës were privileged beyond many youngsters of their own age. And it was during these years that the children's secret and imaginative worlds were created, leading on to their powerful writing skills. These worlds were a strange combination of fantasy mixed with an odd interjection of fact culled from their daily lives, illustrating how these creations were far more than mere childish thoughts. In fact, they governed the inner and creative lives of the sisters and their brother Branwell right up until adult years.

Sketches, maps and the introduction of real-life characters such as Napoleon, Wellington and Lord Byron are all found in these stories recorded in tiny handwriting in equally tiny books to be read by Branwell's toy soldiers belonging to a mystical land called Angria. They show the emergence of amazing creative abilities which would flower in such novels as Emily's *Wuthering Heights*. When Charlotte was sent away to Roe Head School in Mirfield at the age of fifteen, the younger two girls were thrown together and jointly they created the equally absorbing land of Gondal. Geography, history, poems and romance all found a place, complete with illustrations by the young writers.

Charlotte was the acknowledged leader among the sisters. Diminutive in size and extremely short-sighted, she yet had determination of character, whereas Emily was more of a mystic. Anne was gentle and quiet yet with a surprising streak of tenacity and courage. Branwell too was highly creative with an outstanding intelligence and artistic ability. His young life was undoubtedly marred by the sorrows he had known—only four when his mother died and eight when his two oldest sisters died within weeks of each other. His sad life was ruined by repeated failures, alcohol, immorality and opium.

When Charlotte was given a position as a governess at Roe Head School, Emily, now seventeen, was sent there as a pupil. She had never left home since her brief few months at Cowan Bridge at the age of seven. Ten years had passed since then and Emily found she missed the moors, the freedom and personal privacy of home intensely. The regulations of boarding school life with its loss of all she had loved ran against the grain—she even found herself sharing a bed with another girl at night. The situation was too much for her and she became nervously and physically ill. Charlotte watched her sister with alarm and fearing that she also could die like Maria and Elizabeth arranged for her to go home after only three months at Roe Head. Anne, now sixteen, was sent in her place.

Conscientious and determined to take advantage of the educational opportunity, Anne threw herself into her academic work with dedication and even gained an award for diligent behaviour. But beneath her quiet demeanour a spiritual battle was raging. Sunday by Sunday Anne had sat under her father's evangelical preaching and learnt of God's mercy to the penitent. But here at school she was being taught very differently. Only those who reached a certain standard of behaviour could hope for the forgiveness and grace of God. How could she ever attain such a standard? She fretted and grieved over what appeared to be beyond her grasp. At last her spiritual distress became yet more acute when she also succumbed to an infection. In a letter to a friend Charlotte reported that her sister Anne was 'wretchedly ill'.

In her need Anne at last asked to see the minister of the Moravian church in Mirfield, James de la Trobe. He was alarmed at her condition. 'Her life hung by a thread,' he reported. But his words proved better than any medicine. He records what happened. 'I found her well acquainted with the main truths of the Bible respecting our salvation, but seeing them more through the law than the gospel, more as a requirement from God than his gift in his Son.' But, he continues, 'The words of love from Jesus opened her ear to my words, and she was very grateful for my visits.' He continued, 'Her heart opened to the sweet views of salvation, pardon, and peace in the blood of Christ, and she accepted his welcome to the weary and heavy laden sinner'.

It was probably at this time that Anne wrote the words of a hymn still to be found in many hymnals:

> Oppressed with sin and woe
> a burdened heart I bear,
> opposed by many a mighty foe
> yet will I not despair.

> With this polluted heart,
> I dare to come to thee—
> holy and mighty as thou art—
> for thou wilt pardon me.

Most significantly James de la Trobe could say of Anne, 'Had she died then, I would have counted her his (Christ's) redeemed and ransomed child.' And Anne could conclude her hymn:

> In my Redeemer's name
> I give myself to thee;
> and all unworthy as I am,
> my God will welcome me.

At peace spiritually, Anne soon recovered her health and returned home, glad, no doubt, to have finished at Roe Head. Back in Haworth she and her sisters met their father's new curate, William Weightman, a personable young man of twenty-six. He was popular with all three young women and when each received her first Valentine card she had little doubt as to who had travelled away from Haworth to post it. It would seem that Charlotte was most absorbed in every detail of Weightman's activities, judging by the number of times his name crops up in her letters. Nor was she best pleased when she noticed Weightman gazing at Anne. But in the event the young man died of cholera at the age of twenty-eight, probably contracted when he visited a sick parishioner. Lines written by Anne at the time, show how acutely she too felt the loss:

> And yet I cannot check my sighs—
> thou wert so young and fair,
> more bright than summer morning skies,
> but stern Death would not spare.

I'll weep no more thy early doom,
but O! I still must mourn
the pleasures buried in thy tomb
for they will not return.

Courageously Anne determined to seek employment, knowing that her father's stipend could not support his four adult children living at home. To the incredulity of all her family, she accepted a position in Mirfield as a governess for the children of a wealthy couple, the Inghams. Living in a mansion known as Blake Hall, in luxury Anne that could only dream of, she had the two children in her care. Cunliffe was aged six and Mary five. Pampered, rude and ungovernable, they proved resistant to all Anne's best efforts. She was forbidden to correct or punish her young charges, and as they refused to work Anne made little progress. Not surprisingly she was dismissed in a matter of months.

Anne was not slow, however, to seek another appointment as a governess and in 1840, now twenty years of age, she found a prestigious position in a hamlet near York, Thorp Green. Employed by a wealthy vicar, Edmund Robinson and his wife, Anne's task was to teach their three older girls, Lydia, Elizabeth and Mary, aged fourteen, thirteen and twelve with their only son Edmund, aged eight. Although also spoilt and demanding, at least the children were old enough to respond much better to Anne's teaching and after a rocky start the job went much better than at Blake Hall.

Edmund Robinson, a chronic invalid, was in his mid-forties, whereas his wife Lydia was younger, vivacious and flighty. All went well for several years and Anne accompanied the family on their regular holidays to Scarborough, growing to love the bracing sea air. In the meantime, her brother Branwell, who had lost job after job mainly through his heavy drinking and addiction to opium, was unemployed yet again. It was then that Anne suggested that he could join her as a tutor to the Robinson's son who was now twelve. This was agreed, but before long a serious situation began to develop as Branwell became more and more familiar with his employer's wife, the capricious Lydia Robinson. With his history of sexual misdemeanour, Branwell's relationship with Mrs Robinson was distressing Anne. Foreseeing what was coming, she suddenly resigned her position at Thorp Green and returned home. Branwell carried on but it would appear that the situation worsened and suddenly his amours came to light. Edmund Robinson angrily sacked him, forbidding him ever to have any further contact with any member of his family. The disgrace was complete.

In 1845 the Brontë sisters were all unemployed. How could they earn their keep? It was at this time that Charlotte discovered some poems Emily had written. Emily was furious at first, but when Charlotte suggested seeking a publisher she was gradually won round. Anne admitted that she too had written verse and Charlotte agreed, though reluctantly, that Anne's lines had 'a sweet sincere pathos of their own'. With the addition of her own work, Charlotte oversaw the publication of the collection, but knowing the prejudice against women writers the sisters published under the pseudonyms of Currer, Ellis and Acton Bell. Sadly, the publication was a disaster, with only two copies of the first edition being sold, leaving the sisters' ambitions in the dust.

If poetry would not sell, then they would try their hand at novels. Long years of imaginative writing during childhood had prepared them well for such a venture. We can imagine the three seated around the table in the Haworth vicarage each working diligently, sharing their thoughts with each other. Charlotte's first novel was called *The Professor*, but although she sent it to numerous publishers, each sent it back with the same curt refusal. Meanwhile Anne was working on a narrative entitled *Agnes Grey* which describes the experiences of a young well-educated woman setting out on her first job as a governess. Vividly portraying the degrading circumstances faced by Agnes Grey, Anne was in reality recounting her own experiences both with the children at Blake Hall and at Thorp Green. This work is therefore largely autobiographical.

To her astonishment, a publisher, Thomas Newby, accepted the work—doubtless to Charlotte's discomfort, who could never quite believe her youngest sister's exceptional abilities. Published in 1847, and bound together with Emily Brontë's *Wuthering Heights* under her pseudonym Ellis Bell, it proved highly popular and also controversial, arousing not a little curiosity as to who Acton and Ellis Bell might be. The mystery deepened when a different publisher accepted Charlotte's second novel, *Jane Eyre*, under the pseudonym Currer Bell—a novel which immediately received the highest accolades.

Meanwhile Anne was working on a second novel: *The Tenant of Wildfell Hall*, arguably the most courageous of all the Brontë novels. Published in 1848 this book cut across all the norms and protocol of nineteenth-century Regency society in terms of its treatment of women. Married women had no rights at the time and were wholly subject to their husband's whims and control, with no say over the futures of their own children. Anne's heroine, Helen Huntingdon, was married to a drunken, immoral and abusive wretch who was intent on corrupting their only child. Eventually she flees and remains in hiding with the boy. This concept shocked society.

Despite Helen's increasing love for a farmer she meets in her exile, she returns to her husband, Arthur, when she hears he is dying. Her single aim is to care for him sacrificially and to speak to him of a God of mercy and forgiveness who can save his soul from hell. In the pages of this powerfully written novel, Anne's own Christian faith shines out in her descriptions of the final tragic scenes of her husband's life. Arthur begs Helen to plead with God on his behalf. Her reply is significant: 'It cost the blood of an incarnate God, perfect and sinless in himself, to redeem us from the bondage of the evil one—let him plead for you now.' Arthur's last words give Helen some hope of his eternal state. And like all good novels the book has a satisfying end as Helen marries her farmer lover.

But Anne suffered for her audacity by the criticisms heaped on the author of such a book. Cruel things were said, although no one knew for sure whether Acton Bell was a man or a woman. A poem she wrote reflects her inner feelings.

> Believe not those who say
> the upward path is smooth,
> lest thou should'st stumble in the way
> and faint before the truth.
>
> Be this thy constant aim,
> thy hope, thy chief delight;
> what matter who should whisper blame,
> or who should scorn or slight;
>
> If but thy God approve,
> and if, within thy breast,
> thou feel the comfort of his love,
> the earnest of his rest.

But hardest of all was the disapproval of her own sister, Charlotte. In terms of the drunken orgies of Helen Huntingdon's husband, the descriptions were too like the conduct of their own brother Branwell for comfort. Writing about *The Tenant of Wildfell Hall*, Charlotte said, 'The book has faults of execution and faults of art … For my part, I consider the subject unfortunately chosen—it was one the author was not qualified to handle …' And later she would forbid a reprint, adding, 'The choice of subject was an entire mistake.'

This is understandable in the light of Branwell's subsequent three years after Thorp Green. He was unable to gain any further meaningful employment, was repulsed in his subsequent advances to Lydia Robinson following her husband's death and his addiction to drink and opium mastered him. It all rendered him a pathetic and impoverished man. Anne's book was actually published in the summer of 1848, which was before the family realised that in addition to his profligate lifestyle Branwell was also physically ill, having contracted tuberculosis. When his condition became obvious it was too late for any medication. In September 1848 Patrick Brontë knelt at Branwell's bedside, pleading with God for his son's soul. The dying man whispered 'Amen' to his father's intercession, and added, 'In all my past life I have done nothing either great or good.' Twenty minutes later he died. He was thirty-one.

The following few months make incredibly sad reading as first Emily herself died in December 1848 and then Anne the following June. Both young women had contracted tuberculosis— a disease that ravaged society in the nineteenth century. Emily, a tough and determined spirit in a frail body, would not recognise that she was ill and stubbornly refused any medical help. Even to her last evening she struggled to feed her beloved dog, Keeper, and to dress herself the next morning as usual. By two o'clock that afternoon death had conquered her brave spirit.

Grieving and weak from the double loss, Anne had suffered a severe bout of influenza. As the weeks passed she was not gaining strength and in her heart she knew she also was dying. Unlike Emily she meekly accepted all the medical remedies of the day such as bleeding and blistering but they were all ineffectual. One thing she asked—one strand of hope—that if she could be taken to Scarborough the bracing sea air might well improve her condition. Charlotte, possibly shrinking at the prospect of losing Anne as well, refused, until Patrick Brontë intervened and insisted that she be taken. But that was not until May 1849 and the delay cost Anne dear.

Travelling by train to Scarborough on 24 May together with Charlotte and her close friend Ellen Nussey, they booked rooms overlooking the sea where Anne was able to sit watching the ebb and flow of the tides. She took short walks when she felt able, but had little time left. Yet all her thoughts were for others. Again and again she said, 'Take courage, Charlotte, take courage,' and begged Ellen to be a sister to Charlotte in her place. On 28 May, when the end was very close, a doctor was summoned. Anne asked him how long he thought she might live. He admitted that the end was near and was astonished at her tranquillity. 'It is not you who can give me ease,' she told him, 'but soon all will be well through the merits of our Redeemer.' He later said that in all his experience he had never seen a deathbed like it. Conscious to the last, Anne Brontë died 'calmly and gently' at two o'clock that afternoon. She was buried the next day on the hillside overlooking the bay she had loved.

Writing of Anne's death Charlotte recorded that 'She died without severe struggle, resigned, trusting in God ... deeply assured that a better existence lay before her. She believed, she hoped, and declared her belief with her last breath.' She was twenty-nine: she had not lived in vain.

3. Kit Calvert: Wensleydale Cheese

When Nick Park's endearing clay animations, Wallace and his pet dog Gromit, discovered the delicate flavour of Wensleydale Cheese, the brand became their immediate favourite. Not only was it delicious but it made Wallace's face look 'round and toothy'—an important asset as far as he was concerned. Undoubtedly these highly enjoyable clay animations did much to popularise Wensleydale Cheese and even add to its success.

One variety in particular has gained favour with the cheese-loving public. 'Have you ever tried Kit Calvert Wensleydale Cheese?' I asked a friend the other day and immediately received a very positive answer. 'Yes, it is delicious,' she said. The internet adds to its virtues in these words: 'Kit Calvert is a lovingly handcrafted buttery, creamy textured cheese. A cheese celebrating the father of Wensleydale Cheese 'Kit Calvert', who helped to save the Wensleydale Creamery from closure in 1935.'

But who was Kit Calvert and what is his story? Certainly in any book on Yorkshire men and women, this interesting character deserves a place. Born in 1903 in Burtersett, just to the east of Hawes in the Yorkshire Dales, Christopher Thomas Calvert, known as Kit, was the eldest of three boys. He came from an impoverished family and tells us in vivid terms about his home circumstances. His father was a quarryman earning eighteen shillings a week—which had to cover the rent of the home and feed the family. In addition, they kept a few hens, a gander and five geese. On special occasions when the eggs had fetched a good price the boys were able to enjoy a whole egg each, but normally half an egg had to suffice. Each spring the geese laid a clutch of eggs which were allowed to hatch, the goslings being sold to finance the boys' clothes. But one year the old gander had suffered an injury and every egg the geese laid proved infertile. Kit never forgot the shame of having nothing new to wear to the annual Sunday School Anniversary.

To help meet family expenses, young Kit went out to work at the age of twelve. Growing up through the dark days of the First World War, he took on odd jobs at the local farms, tending cattle and caring for sheep at lambing time. But Kit was no ordinary farm labourer. Over the years he was selected for several satisfactory jobs. Wages might have been small, but he was learning all the time. After watching a cattle auction in progress Kit began to take a keen interest in the values of the animals and in 1931 at the age of twenty-eight he took up farming in his own right, buying and selling his stock of lambs and cattle at auction. Shorthorn cattle proved an excellent purchase: tough beasts, they were suitable for either dairy or meat, but produced milk of exceptionally high quality.

These were the hard days of the Great Depression during the late 1920s and early 1930s. Kit's first experiences were discouraging as he saw the price of his lambs plummet year after year until he found it more profitable to sell them individually as meat. It was also hard to obtain a good price for the milk from his cows for a surplus was being produced nationwide. Turning excess milk into cheese seemed the best option but many farmers went bankrupt and Kit himself knew times of severe difficulty as other farmers could often pay 'nowt' for their purchases. At last in 1933 with the Depression at its height, Kit Calvert, with the help of several others, agreed to buy out a bankrupt cheese-making business which owed him £680 for milk purchased during the previous six months—a colossal sum for those days. Employing the firm's senior cheese maker and two of his staff, Kit started a cheese-making business which would one day become the Wensleydale Creamery. He could only pay his men a pittance of a wage at first, but that was better than bankruptcy.

Not long after came an event which turned Kit into a hero among the Dalesmen. In severe difficulties himself he had considered closing down, but had heard that the Milk Marketing Board had just been established and might be persuaded to do a deal with him. Calling a meeting in the Town Hall, Kit drove a fierce bargain with the Board for he was no soft combatant. Good terms were struck for his milk and cheese, enabling Calvert, in his position as manager, to provide employment for a number of Dalesmen. Even Kit worked without pay for the first year, but in 1935, with the help of others, he managed to buy the business back from the Milk Marketing Board, an event that saw the real beginning of the Wensleydale Creamery, called at first, Wensleydale Dairy Products Ltd.

A man of originality of thought, Kit stumbled on a novel and profitable method to dispose of the whey left over from turning five hundred gallons of milk each day into cheese. Normally it was discarded as a waste product, but Kit found that pigs loved it. Buying the pigs on credit, he fattened them up, each pig drinking three to four gallons of whey a day. He then offered them back to the farmer from whom he had purchased them, making almost £1,500 profit at the end of the first year, a considerable sum in the 1930s.

But Kit Calvert made another discovery at about this time, one that sprang from a seemingly trivial event: a discovery of far more critical importance than establishing the Wensleydale Creamery. As he walked along Main Street into Hawes from his village home in Burtersett one day, Kit saw a piece of paper bowling along the road in the wind. Curious about most things in life, Kit stopped and picked it up. To his surprise it was a religious tract. Who could have dropped this? As we have seen, Kit and his family had strong links with the Congregational Chapel in Hawes, having attended services there since a small child. But as he read the tract he discovered something he had never grasped before: that he, Kit Calvert, needed someone to save him from his sins—even the Lord Jesus Christ by his death on the cross. And Kit responded to what he read with a sincere heart.

Although his spiritual conversion became the revolutionary point in his life, it always remained a very private affair, too personal to share with any but a few friends. The result, however, was far from private. Now, in addition to establishing the Creamery, Kit gave much time and energy to serving the Saviour and supporting the ministry in the Congregational Chapel.

Before long he became an avid student of the Bible; the writer of a short account of Kit's life called him 'a devout Christian of the old type'. By this he meant that Kit believed in the divine inspiration of Scriptures and that his heart's trust in Christ as his Saviour and God was both firm and sincere, resulting in an earnest evangelicalism. This was in sharp contrast to the trend in many of the churches of his day. Kit's most significant contribution to the chapels in Hawes, Gayle, Ledbury, and even Swaledale and beyond was as a lay preacher. This often involved long treks each Sunday. We learn that services at these country chapels were lively warm affairs frequently interrupted by shouts of 'Hallelujah, Praise the Lord,' and 'save 'em'.[1]

With a great love for the broad Yorkshire dialect, unintelligible at times to the uninitiated, his preaching rang out in no uncertain tones. Quoting the incident in John's gospel chapter 21 where

---

[1] Much material for this account is drawn from W R Mitchell's small book, *Kit Calvert, Yorkshire Dalesman,* Castleburg 2003.

Christ calls out to his disciples who had been fishing all night on the Lake of Galilee without any success. Calvert renders the conversation in these words: 'Lads, hey ye caught owt?' Th'shooted back, 'Nowt.' So he sez, 'Kest yer net ower t'reet side ev t'booat an' y'ill git a catch.'[2]

Not only did he preach in the local dialect but he translated long passages of Scripture into words that his fellow Yorkshire men would readily understand. Psalm 23 was rendered in this way:

> The Lord is my shipperd,
> Ah'll want fer nowt.
> He lets m'bassock i' t' best pastures
> an' taks m' bi't watter side whar o's wyet an' peeacful.
> He uplifts m'soul an' maks things seea easy
> 'at Ah can drew w'ats reet an' gloryfy His name.
> Evan if Ah cu't' deeaths deursteead,
> Ah's nut bi freetend, fer He'll bi' wi' me.
> His creuk an' esh plant'll uphold me
> Thu puts on a good meeal afoor me,
> reet anenst them' at upbrraids me.
> Thu ceuls me heead wi' oil
> an' Ah'v meeat an' drink t' spar'
> Seurlie Thi goodniss an' mercy
> 'al bi mine fer o' t' days o' mi life,
> an ah'll beleng t' t'hoose o' the Lord fer ivver.

With such delightful rendering of a dialect that is becoming rare in these days, such words are a historical as well as a biblical treasure.

Kit Calvert was a man of many interests, in addition to the booming Wensleydale Creamery. It may be surprising to learn that considering his impoverished childhood, he had a passionate

---

[2] *'Children, do you have any fish?' They answered him 'No'. He said to them, 'Cast your net on the right side of the boat and you will find some.'* (ESV)

love of books. At nine years of age he had begged his father for one thing: a *Collins Dictionary*, on sale for a shilling. With the family income amounting to only eighteen shillings a week, it was a major sacrifice for Moss Calvert—but for Kit's sake he purchased the book. This was the start of a collection of books of all types—a collection that amounted to over five thousand volumes. Stacked crazily from floor to ceiling with the delightful, if stale, smell of old books, we may wonder what his patient wife thought of it. Not only was it books that Kit collected. It takes little imagination to visualise his wife's reaction when the fourth piano was moved into the home, this time a grand piano.

It must have been some relief to her when in 1951 Kit eventually set up a small bookshop in Hawes, a shop that is still going today. He gave away as many books as he sold, only hoping he made enough profit to cover his tobacco, for he was rarely seen without his old clay pipe. 'You can have anything you like for a bob (shilling),' he would say, 'and if you don't think it's worth a bob then give me a tanner (sixpence).' If no one was in attendance at the shop, customers were asked to leave the money in an old tin —a tin that was eventually replaced by a burglar-proof container nailed to the table. By 1965 Kit had accumulated about a thousand books on the Yorkshire dialect alone.

In the meantime, the Wensleydale Creamery had flourished to such an extent that the Milk Marketing Board expressed an interest in repurchasing it. Kit was nearly sixty by this time and was concerned for the future of the Creamery. Feeling that this was the best way to secure the business, and ensure employment for the nearly sixty staff, a price of £500,000 was agreed, with Kit himself persuaded to stay on as manager. Not until 1971 when he was sixty-eight did Kit eventually retire from the Creamery.[3]

---

[3] In May 1992 the Milk Marketing Board decided to transfer the Wensleydale Creamery to Lancashire. Not surprisingly this was highly unpopular and some ex-managers managed to club together to buy it back and by November the Creamery was back in business in Hawes where it now remains and flourishes.

He was now in a position to buy a house in Hawes, one known as Springbank. One feature that attracted him to the property was the fact that it had an acre of ground in front of the house. During the Second World War the Army had secured use of the plot and had built nine large Nissen huts on the site. The purchase of this property enabled Kit Calvert to fulfil another of his life ambitions—to provide a playground for the children of Hawes. Demolishing the huts but retaining their concrete bases, Kit was able to erect areas for swings, roundabouts and many other facilities for local youngsters. It is delightful to think of the old man, pipe in mouth and wearing his old bowler hat, watching the children at play in what amounted to his front garden.

The rest must be quickly told. In 1975 Kit's long-suffering and faithful wife died. They had been married for forty-four years and he missed her sorely. Two years later came an honour which Kit could never have anticipated. The year 1977 commemorated the Silver Jubilee of the reign of Queen Elizabeth II and Kit Calvert was nominated to receive an MBE for his services to his local community. A photo is extant showing this quarryman's son arrayed in pinstripe trousers and coat tails, complete with grey waistcoat and top hat displaying the red and gold cross of a Member of the British Empire—an honour indeed.

But in 1984 Kit Calvert received a far greater reward: greater than establishing the Wensleydale Creamery, greater than his MBE from the hands of the Queen Mother, for he was received into the glory of heaven and heard the words of the Saviour, 'Well done, good and faithful servant.'[4]

---

[4] At his request his coffin was carried on a cart drawn by his old pony, Dolly, the very same pony which appears in the James Herriot films, *All creatures great and small.*

4. John Nelson:
the stonemason preacher

In June 2016 a tragedy brought the village of Birstall, near Leeds, to public attention. Jo Cox, Labour Member of Parliament for the Batley and Spen constituency, was brutally and senselessly murdered as she went about her parliamentary duties. Happily, Birstall may also be remembered for other significant events in its history. Formerly noted as a prosperous village distinguished for its cloth industry, it is now virtually swallowed up in the Leeds/Bradford complex. And it was here that John Nelson, eldest son of a stonemason was born in 1707.

John's father can be best described as a God-fearing man, one who carefully taught his children from the Bible, though he himself had only a sketchy understanding of the great truths he was teaching. John was a serious boy and little did his father guess that his ten-year-old was deeply troubled by some of the things he was telling him. One day as the child sat listening to his father reading to him from the last book of the Bible, the Book of Revelation, John began to tremble. *And I saw a great white throne and him that sat thereon, from whom the heaven and the earth fled away* ... intoned his father, *and the books were opened, and another book was opened which is the Book of life* ...

'A great white throne'? thought John, 'a Book of life'? The little boy could bear no more. He plugged his fingers in his ears but could still hear his father reading on about a dreadful Day of Judgement which was coming. At last John fell on his face and began to cry uncontrollably. The thought of such a day of reckoning terrified him. Nonplussed by his child's distress, John's father had no answers. Nor did anyone in Birstall. Who was there who could tell the boy that not only is there a Day of Judgement but also that God has a plan of mercy through Christ to save men, women and children from such judgement?

As he matured John became an able stonemason like his father, but still could not shake off his early fears. He speaks of experiencing 'a hell in my mind' as he joined with his peers in the excesses of youth. Were there no answers? A girl's pretty face proved a constant snare to him. Perhaps if he could find a good-looking young woman to marry that would curb his giddy lifestyle and bring him peace of conscience. He prayed that God would provide such a girl and not long afterwards he spotted Martha. Never before had John Nelson seen this young woman, but he was convinced that she was the girl for whom he had prayed. Shortly afterwards John and Martha were married, but his problems remained unresolved. Perhaps if he found work further afield he could shake off the temptations that baffled him. But as soon as he returned home he fell back into his old excesses as he met with his former friends.

At last John Nelson decided he must move to London, leaving Martha and their two children in Yorkshire. Unknown to him God's time for this troubled man—now in his early forties, was close. Once there, he tried church after church without success. From no pulpit did he hear any message telling of the forgiveness of sins. Then he learnt of a strange new preacher—actually an Oxford don—who was doing the unthinkable—preaching to vast crowds on the common land that lay beyond the walls of London. John lost no time in joining the throng.

The result is best told in his own words:

> As soon as Mr John Wesley got upon the stand, he stroked back his hair and turned his face toward where I stood, and I thought fixed his eyes upon me

... and when he did speak I thought his whole discourse was aimed at me. When he had done I said: 'This man can tell the secrets of my heart, but he hath not left me there, for he hath showed the remedy—even the blood of Jesus.'

John Nelson had reached a turning point. He struggled on for a few weeks—trying to read the Bible, then, taunted by his old companions, he was dragged back to the ale houses. As soon as he had a little liquor inside him, he gave in to all his old weaknesses and especially when an immoral woman met him and lured him into an illicit act. Did he even think of his Martha far off in Yorkshire?

Back in his rooms John Nelson was desperate. Falling on his knees, he cried out, 'Lord, save me or I perish.' He determined that he would neither eat nor drink until he had 'found the kingdom of God'. Vehemently he cried out for forgiveness until he virtually lost his voice. Then in silence he waited, kneeling before the Lord. He tells us he was 'like a criminal before the Judge.' Then he said, 'Lord, thy will be done. Damn or save.' That moment he saw the truth at last. Jesus Christ had been crucified, paying the price for John Nelson's sins. Rising from his knees he felt a tremendous release from the tormenting fears of years and was filled with a calm and sweet peace. John Nelson was a changed man.

But trouble was in store. Bubbling over with enthusiasm and the joy of forgiveness, John spoke freely to all his associates of his new-found joys. His landlady was furious and threatened to put him on the street; his employers wished to terminate his contract because he would not work on Sundays, and his former friends boycotted him. Eager now to get back to Martha, John wrote to tell her of the amazing change in his life.

While Martha was pleased to hear that John was coming home, she was not at all sure about the news he was sharing. In the event she became acutely embarrassed. Not only did John tell everyone of what had transformed his life, he fearlessly pointed out the glaring sins he saw in his own former behaviour and that of his friends and associates. Panic stricken, Martha was afraid to leave her house for fear of her neighbours' tongues. 'I wish he had stayed in London,' she thought miserably. At last she could bear it no longer and issued an ultimatum: unless John would stop offending everybody, she would no longer live with him.

Even worse would follow from Martha's point of view. Daily her little home was packed with anxious people who wished to hear this strange new message that John had discovered—that it was possible to know one's sins were forgiven for Christ's sake. Within three weeks of Nelson's return, seventeen of his friends and neighbours had been converted. But not Martha. Despite his protestations of even stronger love for her, she cried in distress 'My happiness is over. According to you I am a child of the devil and you are a child of God. I cannot stay with you.'

Daily John Nelson gave himself to fasting and prayer for his wife. 'I believe God will hear my prayer and convert your soul,' he assured her, 'and make you a blest companion for me in the way to heaven.' Then Martha became dangerously ill. In her utter weakness, facing possible death, she realised that unless Christ intervened and saved her soul she would perish forever. Crying out at last to God for mercy and healing, she knew almost instantly that he had granted both. From that moment Martha began to recover, and she too would become a courageous follower of Jesus Christ, often enduring suffering herself as a result.

West Yorkshire provided a ready mission field for John Nelson. Little gospel truth had yet penetrated this part of the country. After a long day's work hammering, chiselling and shaping stones, John rushed home, and without stopping to change his clothes, hurried off to where expectant people were gathering to hear him preach. They listened avidly as he told of forgiveness of sins for those who repent and cry out to God for mercy. But it was not all plain sailing. Enflamed by cheap gin, the crowds were often abusive for who likes to hear that their life-style is unacceptable with God? Missiles would fly through the air, often striking the preacher on the head. Sometimes burning fireworks were flung at him.

Martha too suffered. On one occasion she was returning from Wakefield with a few other women when she was suddenly aware that she was being followed. Heavily pregnant at the time, she realised she was in danger. As she reached a narrow gate she heard a coarse voice calling out, 'You are John Nelson's wife—and here you shall die.' Kicked and mercilessly beaten by a gang of thugs, Martha staggered home, and sadly gave birth to a dead baby. She never fully recovered from this assault.

The vicar of Birstall was angered at Nelson's intrusion onto his 'patch' and had little difficulty in arranging for the resolute preacher to be press-ganged into the Army especially as the Second Jacobite Rebellion was in full swing. For ten weeks John was held, first in custody and then in military service. Undaunted, he continued to preach to his fellow soldiers until the rebellion was crushed and John was set at liberty.

Even then Nelson's sufferings were by no means over. On one occasion a mob near Leeds determined to drown the intrepid preacher. Grabbing him from behind, they attempted to fasten a halter round his neck and drag him to a nearby river. As they fumbled to fasten the halter, these perpetrators panicked when a local constable appeared on the scene. Soon after this another attempt to kill Nelson very nearly succeeded as a colossal man leapt on him, threw him to the ground and stamped on him relentlessly. With his huge weight he soon crushed his victim until Nelson lay apparently lifeless. 'I have killed your preacher,' the assailant declared in triumph as he dragged the still form to a nearby croft. As some of John's friends gathered in grief around the inert body they discovered to their joy that he was still alive. Moving him to one of their homes, they tended him until he was strong enough to return to Martha.

Gradually the intensity of persecution lessened as the effects of the revival of gospel preaching took hold of men and women, changing lives and homes in Birstall, Leeds, all West Yorkshire and far beyond. But Nelson knew that the situation could change again and was anxious for Birstall to have a chapel of its own where anyone denied access to a local church could meet. Returning to his brick making, he hewed and crafted stones and helped to construct a handsome chapel. By 1750 the building was almost finished, and in August that year William Grimshaw of Haworth preached the first sermon. Later John Wesley himself would preach there. In 1751 a small study adjacent to the chapel, one where Nelson could read and pray, was completed; it still stands today as a listed building. The main chapel itself, now converted into office buildings, retains its connection with the early Methodists and is called Wesley House.

The sufferings John Nelson had endured had taken a heavy toll on his health. By the age of sixty-two he could hardly walk and had to lean on another man to hold him steady as he preached. But the well-loved preacher struggled on for a further five years; even the sight of his weakness filled his hearers with affection and gratitude as they noted with deep satisfaction that his messages were as tender, warm and powerful as ever they had been despite his obvious pain.

The end came suddenly. Stricken with severe stomach pains as he returned home from a preaching engagement in 1774, it was evident to Martha that John would shortly leave her. In fact, only two hours later God called his courageous servant away from the toils and pain of all his labours and trials. And his funeral! Can there ever have been one like it? Thousands lined the route along which the coffin was carried, weeping and singing hymns composed by Charles Wesley as they went. Genuinely and deeply loved, John Nelson was buried in the graveyard of Birstall parish church. And a mere two months later his long-suffering wife Martha followed him to the land of joy where sorrow and infirmity is gone forever.

5. Samuel Marsden: apostle to the Maori

A courageous man is standing not far from the beach in the Bay of Islands, New Zealand. He is mounted on a pulpit made from a canoe and in front of him stand ranks of wild-looking Maori tribesmen, many of them cannibals, scantily dressed and watchful, spears at the ready. The date is December 25—Christmas Day— 1814 and the sturdy Yorkshire man who is about to preach is Samuel Marsden. Historically, the significance of this scene is incalculable, for this was the very first time that the Christian gospel was being preached in that land.

Samuel Marsden was born in Farsley, Yorkshire, a village now swallowed up in the Leeds/Bradford conurbation, but once an attractive hamlet with a long history that even found a place in the Domesday Book. Here Thomas Marsden, a small-time farmer, and Bathsheba his wife lived out their quiet days with their large family around them. Samuel, who was born in 1764, was their seventh child. Life may have seemed uneventful enough, but in fact these were highly significant days in the story of Christianity in Britain. The preaching of John and Charles Wesley, George Whitefield and a host of lay preachers had been stirring the country to its depths, proclaiming the truths of the evangelical gospel. William Grimshaw, a powerful preacher from Haworth who had died the year before Samuel was born, was once a frequent visitor to the Leeds area.

How Bathsheba and Thomas Marsden were themselves touched by the message which these travelling evangelists brought we do not know. It might have been through the stonemason-preacher, John Nelson from Birstall, or through Benjamin Ingham from Ossett or even William Grimshaw himself. But we know that these godly parents had the wisdom to send their young son Samuel to Hull Grammar School for his education. Dr Joseph Milner was headmaster at the time, a brilliant man and even more significantly, a man deeply touched by the evangelical revival. Under his influence the city of Hull had been transformed by the gospel, especially as a result of his dual role both as headmaster and lecturer at the large city church of Holy Trinity.

During the time Samuel Marsden was in Hull, Rowland Hill —the popular preacher from Surrey Chapel in London—could describe the city as 'a garden of the Lord'. Church attendance had grown astonishingly and over two thousand people would often attend the midweek meetings of the churches. It is not surprising then that when Samuel Marsden left Hull the young man clearly shared that same deep passion for the gospel and was eager to see lives changed by it.

Marsden returned to Yorkshire but not to Farsley as his parents had died. Instead the young man went to live in nearby Horsforth with his uncle who was a blacksmith. Working diligently during the day both in farming and helping his uncle, Marsden spent his evenings travelling round the nearby villages, preaching wherever he had opportunity. Then came a big change in his circumstances. In 1790 when he was about twenty-five he received an unexpected grant from the Elland Society, newly-formed to provide financial support to hopeful young evangelical men, allowing them to go to university to train for the ministry.

So to Cambridge Marsden went and there studied diligently. But before he could graduate there came another astonishing development in Samuel Marsden's life.

Possibly due to the influence of William Wilberforce, MP for Hull whom he had known from his days in the city, Marsden was appointed to be assistant chaplain of the British Colony in New South Wales, Australia. England was in the habit of dumping its unwanted citizens in that far off land and Marsden was to be given spiritual responsibility for these troubled and often hardened men and women. To leave his Yorkshire home and travel to a distant and unknown land was hazard enough, but to do so on a ship packed with convicts and criminals must have been fearsome at best. Before venturing on such an enterprise Marsden had the wisdom to ask a courageous young woman to marry him. He had known Elizabeth Tristan from his Hull days and with her agreement they began a shared life of adventure and sorrows.

A stormy five-month voyage amongst angry and bitter convicts was not an easy backdrop for Elizabeth's first pregnancy and the birth of her daughter. But at last, in March 1794, the young couple arrived in Australia—land of opportunity, but also of extraordinary sorrows and misunderstandings for the Marsdens. Stationed at Parramatta not far from Sydney, Samuel and Elizabeth set up their first home, ministering to his unwilling and often unresponsive congregation.

Things became worse when the thirty-year-old chaplain was also appointed as magistrate for the colony. This was a common practice in England at that time but it is hard to imagine two more diverse roles. Marsden was required both to preach to his congregation and also to sentence them for their misdemeanours. In this dual capacity he was scarcely likely to win many converts, especially as some of the penalties he imposed for wrongdoing were considered over-severe at times. History has dealt harshly with Marsden over this with his reputation sadly besmirched, both in his lifetime and frequently since. Some of this stems from petty jealousies but added to this was a dislike of Marsden's high Christian standards and clear preaching which was fervent, and challenging.

Seething with resentment, some of the convicts plotted against their chaplain-judge. One day while walking along the bank of a river, Marsden saw a convict suddenly plunge into the water. Waving his arms and struggling, the man appearing to be drowning. Without a second thought Marsden plunged in after him and tried to save him. The convict, however, attempted to hold Marsden's head under water in order to drown him. A desperate tussle ensued. Eventually Marsden succeeded in reaching the shore safely, dragging the convict with him, whereupon the wretched man, overcome with remorse, confessed his dreadful motive. Angry because of the preacher's emphasis on sin, he had determined upon revenge. He knew that the sight of a drowning man would summon the instant help of one who would defy any danger in the discharge of duty. So he had thrown himself into the stream confident he could drown Marsden and then escape. This convict came penitently to the Saviour, became a faithful Christian, and spoke freely of Jesus Christ who had saved his own soul.

Much of the land around Parramatta was wild and barren and its population of migrants and convicts sometimes reduced to near starvation. But with the eye of both a farmer and a business man, Marsden realised the great potential of agriculture. Availing himself of a grant of land and employing some of the convicts, he began cultivation. Within a few years he had purchased more land, and soon woodland was cleared, roads built and crops harvested. His small flock of sheep reared for wool and meat quickly multiplied. Much of the proceeds were used to better the lives of those among whom he worked. He built schools for the children and in 1799 initiated the building of a church in Parramatta to be called St John's. Made originally from the materials of two derelict huts, the elegant twin spires of St John's Cathedral now break the Parramatta skyline—a memorial to Samuel Marsden.

In 1807 Marsden returned to England to ask for more funds and workers. He was especially troubled about the state of the women convicts, exiled from England for prostitution and petty crimes, sometimes only stealing to feed their families. Degraded and desperate, these women needed shelter and protection. Marsden pleaded their needs with the British government to enable him to build satisfactory living accommodation and provide employment for them.

Before he sailed Marsden had packed into the hold of the ship a dozen small bales of wool from the sheep he had been rearing in Australia. He knew well the importance of the wool industry in his West Yorkshire home area. Perhaps Australian wool would prove popular in England. Sadly, the texture of his wool aroused little interest, so rather than take it back with him he gave it to a merchant—Thompsons of Horsforth—asking only that some be turned into a black suit for him. Woven in nearby Rawdon, Marsden's black suit looked so impressive that when he attended an interview with King George III, the king admired it highly and asked that he might have a similar suit. In return he gave Marsden five merino sheep from his Windsor estate to take back with him for his Parramatta farms. So began the Australian wool industry on a large scale ending up some ten years later with about fifty one thousand sheep, plus cattle, pigs and horses.

But Samuel Marsden had nobler dreams than wool, farming or even church buildings. He cared passionately for the unreached Maori people of nearby New Zealand. This stay in England from early 1807 to May 1809 prepared the way for establishing a mission to the Maoris. On board ship as he returned to Australia he met a Maori tribesman. Ruatara was an adventurous fellow who had served on a number of European ships but had been fearfully mistreated by Europeans as he served as a crew member. Whipped and robbed of his rightful pay, Ruatara was ill and destitute when Marsden discovered him. During the long voyage Marsden nurtured the friendship, taught Ruatara English and learnt a smattering of Maori in return. Back in Parramatta he gave him shelter and employment and taught him from Scriptures.

A changed man, Ruatara returned to his own tribe in the Bay of Islands, and acted as an ambassador for Marsden, as he tried to dispel their suspicion and antagonism against all white men. This proved of vital importance owing to a fearful disaster that had occurred in 1810. Another Maori chief had been on board an English ship called *The Boyd*. Like Ruatara he too had been disgracefully mistreated. Returning home, he waited for his moment of revenge. When *The Boyd* next anchored near the Bay of Islands, Maori tribesmen swarmed aboard. Attacking passengers and crew alike, they killed and ate sixty-seven of them, saving only two women and a boy as slaves.

In the light of such cannibalism, it is not surprising that the Governor of the New South Wales colony was reluctant to allow Marsden the use of a ship to sail to the Bay of Islands himself to preach the Christian gospel. Instead, with steely determination, this intrepid evangelist saved up from his own resources until he had accumulated enough money to buy a small vessel of his own, one which he named *The Active*.

In October 1814, he and the crew, together with the three other missionaries, and their families, thirty-five in all, set sail for New Zealand. Ruatara had done his work ably. He had spoken well of Marsden, introduced his fellow Maori to the wonders of a crop that could actually be turned into flour to make bread, and told them of a strange animal that white men used that could even carry a man on its back—a horse.

On 14 December 1814 *The Active* cast anchor near the Bay of Islands. As he stepped ashore, a weird scene greeted him. On the hill opposite the landing place a band of naked warriors, armed with clubs and spears, occupied a commanding position. After a pause a Maori chief stepped forward flourishing a red mat and crying, '*Haromai!*' which means 'come here'. Then these armed men advanced. Some wore necklaces made from the teeth of their slaughtered foes, while others had strings of money they had plundered from their victims, murdered on that very beach. Seizing their spears, they brandished them, screaming and yelling with savage fury. This unnerving ritual was their war-dance, but these chiefs declared that it meant a welcome to one they considered a friend and a wonder-worker. This latter impression arose in part from the fact that they had never seen a horse before; accordingly, when Marsden brought a horse from the ship, mounted and rode it, the people's amazement knew no bounds.

Speaking through Ruatara as interpreter, Marsden addressed the gathered tribesmen and their chiefs, telling them the object of their visit was to bring peace between the warring tribes, to teach their children, plant crops and build boats. Marsden believed strongly that a degree of civilisation must be brought to a society before the truths of the Christian gospel could take effective root.

With any lingering suspicions calmed, the chiefs and people even accepted an invitation to go aboard *The Active*. The missionaries were in danger, for the Maori far outnumbered them, but trust had now been established. Gifts were exchanged and when all were back on shore Marsden and his fellow missionaries presented the Maori chiefs with horses, cows and sheep. That night the fearless missionary slept among the Maori warriors who lay on the ground each with a spear beside him. 'I did not sleep much,' he says in his journal (which we may add was hardly surprising) and added, 'As I lay awake that night there shone in the skies above me one of the most striking constellations—the Southern Cross. A brilliant diadem of light.' It gave him assurance of God's purposes and grace in that uncertain situation.

Then came that historic Christmas Day, 1814. Ruatara and his friends had everything prepared for that first Christian service on New Zealand soil. He had fenced off half an acre of beach, and used upturned canoes as seats for the mission party. The pulpit from which Marsden was to preach was also made from part of a canoe, covered with cloth.

The 'congregation', consisted of some three to four hundred men scantily dressed, swords and switches still in hand. They stood separated into their different and often antagonistic tribal groups, waiting in wary order. Then Samuel Marsden mounted his makeshift pulpit and began to sing the Old One Hundredth, 'All people that on earth do dwell/sing to the Lord with cheerful voice …'

In respectful astonishment they listened as he told them of those good tidings from the God of heaven sent to the Maori peoples—a message of forgiveness for their past, even for their warring and cannibalism—through the child of Bethlehem, Jesus Christ. *Behold, I bring you good tidings of great joy. Unto you is born this day a Saviour who is Christ the Lord.* Later he wrote in his journal, 'In the above manner the gospel has been introduced into New Zealand, and I fervently pray that the glory of it may never depart from its inhabitants till time shall be no more.'

He was right. Before he left New Zealand several weeks later Marsden was able to buy two hundred acres of land as a permanent base for the three other missionary couples to continue. After an uncertain start the gospel of Jesus Christ took hold of these Maori peoples. Many laid aside their warring habits becoming sincere Christian men and women.

Marsden returned to New Zealand six more times to see the progress of the work. His seventh and last journey through the area was amazing. Now seventy-two years old and far from well, he insisted on visiting his beloved Maori people once more. Wherever he went he was greeted by the Christians with tears of joy, muskets were fired in celebration and some even performed their war-dance. One old chief sat gazing at him for a long time. When reproved, he replied: 'Let me alone. Let me take a long last look, for I shall never see again the one by whose lips God sent to me the blessed news of salvation.' Thousands came to greet him and when he was about to re-embark the Maoris carried him on their shoulders to the ship, a distance of six miles.

Marsden returned to Parramatta and five months later, May 12, 1838, he died. As the end drew near someone asked him if he had hope in Christ. In response he murmured, 'Precious! Precious! Precious!' The last words of a noble Christian. And the flame of the Christian gospel, lit that Christmas Day in 1814 from a pulpit made from a canoe, grew and still shines steadily in New Zealand today.

6. James Hudson Taylor: for love of Christ and China

'If I had a thousand lives, China should have them all. No! Not China, but Christ. Can we do too much for him? Can we do enough for such a precious Saviour?' These words, written by James Hudson Taylor, sum up his life goal. He was a man of single purpose—a man whose every hour was swallowed up in one great passion—to see the gospel of Jesus Christ bringing light and salvation to the Chinese people.

Born on 21 May 1832 at 21 Cheapside in Barnsley, South Yorkshire, Hudson Taylor was the son of James Taylor, a practicing chemist. The building is still a chemist shop but now run by Boots instead. Visitors can be seen reading the plaques outside the shop, one in English, one in Chinese, that commemorate the extraordinary and dedicated life of that Barnsley chemist's son, Hudson Taylor. Perhaps Matthew Arnold had it right in his poem 'The Scholar Gipsy', words that can be fittingly applied to James Hudson Taylor,

> Thou hadst one aim, one business, one desire …
> else hadst thou spent, like other men, thy fire.

And Hudson Taylor's one aim was to reach the thronging millions of China with the gospel of Jesus Christ, a passion that seized him soon after his conversion at the age of seventeen.

To fulfil his aim he would need some medical training and at the age of nineteen he moved to become a medical assistant to Robert Hardey. With little money or means, Taylor devoted himself to serving the poor of the city relying implicitly on God to provide for his needs. In so doing he was consciously preparing himself for a life of faith and service, that he foresaw ahead of him in China. The following year the young man moved to London to begin serious medical training at the Royal London Hospital in Whitechapel.

China was much in the news at that time due to the Anglo-Chinese war fought between 1839 and 1842 and known as the First Opium War—a war in which England had played a far from noble part. With the settlement of the Treaty of Nanking, five ports along the east coast of China were opened up to British trade, awakening great interest in China and the concept that the country was now wide open to Christian missions. Although far from true, this notion led to the founding of the Chinese Evangelisation Society, and young Hudson Taylor was quick to offer himself as their first missionary.

So in September 1853 the twenty-one-year-old Barnsley chemist's son sailed to China, undertaking a challenge of almost staggering proportions and an almost unthinkable voyage for those days, one that took nearly five months. Poverty, dirt, disease and danger awaited him there. Alone in a strange culture and with little grasp of the language, Taylor struggled with fears and doubts, but gradually learnt through his many trials that God never fails his people. Years of lonely toil and travel followed as Hudson Taylor, dressed in a Chinese gown, with his hair scraped back into a pigtail in common with the locals at the time, gave all his energy to evangelism, to starting schools and to giving medical help.

But Hudson was lonely. Now twenty-five he longed for someone to share his life and before long an attractive young teacher in a nearby school caught his eye. Maria Dyer, still only eighteen, was herself a child of missionaries, but had lost both her parents some years earlier and was now under the guardianship of an uncle in England. Described as 'vivacious, witty and intelligent', Maria was also clearly attracted to Hudson. But there was a problem. Her employer at the school, Miss Aldersey, strongly objected to the marriage. She wrote to Maria's guardian, making it quite clear that this impoverished strange-looking man in Chinese dress was a totally unsuitable suitor for Maria, and suggested he refused permission for an engagement to go ahead. The stand-off continued for many months, with little contact between Hudson Taylor and Maria until at last a letter from Maria's guardian arrived, a letter insisting that the girl had the right to choose her marriage partner. He had investigated Taylor's background, he said, and was satisfied by all he discovered. As soon as Maria came of age the wedding could go ahead. In 1858, when Maria had just turned twenty-one, she and Hudson, now twenty-seven, were married—a marriage of deep and inseparable companionship and love, easing Hudson Taylor's burden and sharing his work.

But despite this the young missionary was worn out and his strength clearly failing. At last in 1860 serious illness, thought to be hepatitis, forced the couple to return to England together with their young daughter Grace. Five long years of recuperation followed, but even so they remained years crammed with activity as Hudson Taylor struggled to awaken English missionary societies to the desperate need of China for the gospel. Despite long periods of weakness, he gave himself little rest and sometimes spent up to thirteen hours a day revising his translation of the first Chinese New Testament.

Then came a crisis, a turning point. Still ill and deeply discouraged by the lack of response he discovered on all sides, Hudson Taylor went alone to Brighton for a brief holiday. Imagine the young missionary pacing backwards and forwards on

Brighton's sands deep in thought, his heart yearning for the Chinese people to hear the Christian gospel. Well, if no missionary society was prepared to send men and women to China, perhaps he ought to recruit willing workers himself. The spiritual battle was fierce. Who would finance the endeavour? What if it failed or the conditions proved too hard? Describing the occasion, he wrote, 'In great spiritual agony I wandered out on the sands alone. And there the Lord conquered my unbelief, and I surrendered myself to God for this service.' In an extraordinary act of faith, he prayed that God would provide twenty-two men and women as missionaries, two for each of the eleven inland provinces of China.

And it was a prayer God answered. The China Inland Mission was born. Hearing of the endeavour, some volunteered to go, others to give generously to fund the new mission. In May 1866 sixteen had offered their services and set sail for China together with the Taylor's four young children on the *Lammermuir*, joining the missionary personnel already in the country. Pledging themselves to live without fixed financial support, and each dressed in Chinese clothing, they scattered over many of China's inland provinces and began the lonely and costly work of spreading the Christian gospel in that vast land.

But there were severe trials and setbacks. The death of seven-year-old Grace, Hudson and Maria's delightful eldest child, was followed soon after by the loss of Maria herself from cholera in 1870. It was a bitter blow. In desperate need of someone to care for his young family and to love and support Hudson himself, he married Jennie Faulding the following year. Jennie had sailed on the *Lammermuir* with that first group of missionary volunteers and a noble partnership it proved, lasting until her death in 1904, shortly before that of Hudson Taylor himself in 1905.

Throughout the remaining years of the nineteenth century the numbers offering to serve Christ in China had been steadily increasing, despite setbacks and tragedies. Foremost of these was the massacre of fifty-eight of the missionaries together with twenty-one of their children during the Boxer riots in 1900. The effect of this sorrow on Hudson Taylor, now sixty-eight years of age, was profound, leading to a breakdown in his nervous and physical health.

Much of the latter years of Hudson Taylor's life had been spent campaigning for China's needs in various countries. But he had one deep longing—to return to China himself one last time before he died. And it was a wish God granted. Though frail in body and still grieving over the loss of his well-loved Jennie, the way opened for him to return. With a surprising renewal of strength, Hudson Taylor was able to visit many of the mission stations where the work was established. But during this trip this heroic visionary died unexpectedly and suddenly at the age of seventy-three. In line with his own request he was buried beside his beloved first wife, Maria.

At that time the China Inland Mission was the world's largest Protestant missionary society with over 800 missionaries and 205 mission stations. The society still continues today under the name OMF International and has representatives all over the Far East. Hudson Taylor's story demonstrates what God can do through a man or woman utterly dedicated to his service and to the spiritual needs of others. He can truly be called one of Yorkshire's noblest sons.

7: Fred Mitchell: climbing on track

If the China Inland Mission was born through the vision and courage of a chemist's son from Barnsley named Hudson Taylor, then another chemist, this time from Bradford, also deserves a place among the heroes who laboured and died in the cause of Christian mission in China. His name was Fred Mitchell.

The wooded slopes of Jackson Bridge's famous mile-long hill, venue of the national hill climb for cyclists, must have been a favourite scramble for Fred and his friends. Born in nearby Scholes in 1897, Fred Mitchell spent his childhood in the idyllic Yorkshire village of Jackson Bridge. Brought up in a Methodist family, he regularly sang in the church choir and attended the services. A cocksure, intelligent boy, he won a scholarship to a well-reputed local grammar school at the age of thirteen. Leaving school at sixteen, Fred began to train as a pharmacist in Huddersfield, travelling there each day by rail together with his friend Walter who also had a job in the town.

Then on one occasion an old mill worker accosted the boys as they were about to catch their train, and thrust a Christian tract into Fred's hand. 'Are you saved?' he asked them. Of course they were 'saved', Fred assured Walter. After all, they attended church regularly. But Walter was not convinced, and day after day as they travelled together he posed the same question to his friend, 'Are you really sure we are saved?' Gradually Fred himself grew worried. What did the old mill worker mean? They decided they would visit him and find out how to be certain they were saved. With simplicity and tenderness, the old man worked through the Scriptures with the boys, showing them that however upright they might be, however many times they attended church, this did not make them acceptable in the sight of a holy God. Apart from the death of Christ on the cross, as the sinless Son of God who bore the penalty as a substitute for their sins, they could not hope to be 'saved'.

Still the boys seemed puzzled, even unmoved. 'Why did Jesus cry out "My God, my God, why have you forsaken me?" when he was dying?' posed Fred. With deep passion the old man exclaimed, 'He was forsaken by God because he was bearing our sin—our sin. God cannot look on iniquity.' At that moment Fred understood. Later he was to write, 'It was as if a blind had been drawn up in my soul. The light streamed in. I was saved and knew it. Hallelujah!' The same was true for Walter as these two young men stood at the dawn of a lifetime of service for God. Fired with zeal for others to know what it meant to 'be saved', they began to distribute tracts wherever they could and although he was only seventeen, Fred started to preach in the surrounding villages wherever he had opportunity.

It was 1914. Dark clouds of war were now beginning to gather over Europe and then on 28 July war was declared. But it seemed a distant struggle to Fred as he studied to be a pharmacist in far-off Yorkshire. Nor did anyone think it would last much longer than a few months. But Christmas came and went and it became increasingly evident that any victory over the German forces would be hard won. A wave of patriotism swept over the country as all eligible young men were signing up to join the armed forces. And Fred would soon be eighteen. But he had a major problem. With all the ardour of his Christian commitment he felt it was sinful to take human life—a view he was later to change. Conscientious Objectors were despised, snubbed, even victimised for their views. Fred attempted to join the medical corps, but was unsuccessful. The only option remaining to him as he turned eighteen was to join a non-combatant corp.

As Fred Mitchell, the open-faced, sincere young man from Yorkshire, loaded guns and prepared ammunition for others to fire, he became increasingly troubled. Was there any real difference between what he was doing and actually firing the weapons himself? Then came the Battle of Ypres in August 1915 with the fearsome use of chlorine gas for the first time. Men were gasping and dying in their thousands. Fred knew he could not go on. He disobeyed orders by refusing to comply with the assignment he was given. Death by firing squad could be the penalty for such insubordination. Fred Mitchell was court-martialed but spared that ultimate punishment. Instead he found himself being returned to Britain and hustled through the menacing gates of Wormwood Scrubs prison. And a prisoner he would remain until the end of the war.

With sparse meals, and long hours of isolation, Fred Mitchell might well have been tempted to despair. Instead he saw it as a unique opportunity to read and study his Bible as never before. In fact, it became a period of fundamental importance in his entire life story. He began to read—books he might never have had opportunity to read in the normal busyness of life. Of vital significance was one particular title. Written by A. E. Glover, a missionary in China who had experienced first-hand the horrors of the Boxer Risings of 1900, the book was called *A thousand miles of miracle in China*. The moving account told of the sufferings of Christian missionaries throughout those terrifying days. Hunted mercilessly like wild animals, some fifty-six men and women were tortured and killed along with their children. But more than this, the account also recorded amazing deliverances, narrow escapes and unexpected providences from God that were experienced by some of the missionaries at this time. As Fred later said, 'It stirred my youthful soul to the depths.' A new ambition grew in his heart —he would go to China to help to fill up the depleted ranks brought about by the martyrdom of those brave missionaries.

With the end of the war in 1918 Fred Mitchell was freed and held high hopes that he would soon be able to apply to the China Inland Mission for service in that needy land. But circumstances arose that changed everything. Fred's father was struck down by the devastating flu epidemic that swept thousands to an early grave in a matter of weeks following the end of the war. It is estimated that more died in that epidemic than in the war itself. With no financial support from the government available for widows at that time, this situation made Fred instantly responsible for his mother. The immediate prospect of going to China faded. But the hope of it still burned fiercely in his soul. 'When I am dead,' he once said, 'you will find China written on my heart.'

Not long after qualifying as a pharmacist, Fred Mitchell applied for a post as manager in a chemist shop in nearby Bradford. One pressing reason for his decision was that he had fallen in love with Nellie Heys, an earnest Christian girl whom he had known from childhood days for she too was from Jackson Bridge. If they were to marry they would need a home of their own and a settled income. With a position gained, Fred and Nellie married in 1922.

Although he could not go to China there was much he could do for that distant land. He could pray. And not only did he pray on his own, he also began to organise prayer gatherings for the work of Christian missionaries in China in a number of locations in the Bradford area. He corresponded regularly with the mission headquarters in London to ask for items of concern and to report on the growth of the prayer gatherings. But Fred Mitchell was also an excellent chemist and business man and felt increasingly the need to open his own chemist shop. When he saw a derelict grocer's shop for sale he immediately realised the potential of the disused shop and in 1932 bought the premises. His friends were gloomy. Bradford had fifty chemist shops already: how could Fred hope to compete? But compete he did and in time Fred Mitchell —Chemist became the most sought-after chemist in town. And he dispensed more than medicines—he dispensed wise and kindly counsel as well. A steady stream of anxious men and women made their way into the back of his shop and very often left with good advice plus a tract along with their medical supplies.

But still China held a pre-eminent place in his affections. Again and again he corresponded with mission headquarters to enquire about needs for prayer and to support missionaries financially. Then one day in 1942 a letter dropped through the Mitchells' letter box—one that would change their whole life and Fred's in particular. It was an invitation to him to take up the position of new Home Director of the China Inland Mission—a staggering proposition.

'But I have never even been to China,' objected Fred to his wife Nellie. 'How can I possibly undertake such a position?' The struggle was long and hard. It meant uprooting his family and turning his back on all his professional training—and yet, could it possibly be God's will, the answer to his heart-longings over many years? At last it was Nellie who became convinced that it was God's purpose for him—even though her natural instincts made such a decision hard. With humble dependence on God the stocky Yorkshire chemist sold up his business and moved to Newington Green in North London. Nor was it easy at first. Having been his own boss for many years it was far from trouble-free for Fred Mitchell to consult and work together with others on the major decisions that affected the life of the mission. Gradually over the first months Fred Mitchell learnt to work well in co-operation with others and enjoyed warm relationships with other members of the staff.

Then in 1947 there came at last the fulfilment of his long-cherished desire—a visit to China. He had lived in that distant land in imagination for so long that the strange sights, smells and diet that greeted him seemed almost familiar to him. Yet riding on horseback through rushing rivers and along precipitous mountain ledges at the age of fifty was almost more than the staid Yorkshire man could handle. But best of all was the establishing of warm friendships with the many missionaries for whom he had prayed over many years and this was a privilege that brought him untold joy.

But these were also sad and crucial days for the China Inland Mission. Just two years after his appointment as Home Director the Communist take-over in China brought about a watershed in the life of the Mission. The next two years were tense and difficult as it became increasingly clear that the new government no longer welcomed Christian missionaries in China. Not only were they unwanted, but were becoming an increasing source of embarrassment and potential persecution for the Chinese churches they were serving. Then came the sad day when all missionaries were forced to leave. Fred Mitchell's wisdom and faith during this critical period was of inestimable worth.

But there was hope. As the doors of China slammed shut to Christian missionaries, the prospect of opening opportunities in other South East Asia countries looked increasingly bright. The perspective of the mission had long been summed up in the words 'Have faith in God' and over the impressive entrance to the mission headquarters in Newington Green those four words had been engraved in the stone work. How often must Fred Mitchell have glanced up and read the words as he entered the premises during those demanding days. Astonishingly at the height of the crisis in May 1951 a blackbird actually built her nest over the word 'faith'—a symbol of trust and confidence that no one could miss.

The first missionaries began to settle in Malaysia early in 1952[5] and in April 1953 Fred Mitchell, now fifty-five years of age, paid a visit to the country to encourage the new workers. 'Persevere to the end' was the heart of the message he brought to these missionaries, some recently expelled from China. Twice he chose to preach on the words of the Apostle Paul shortly before his death: I *have fought a good fight, I have finished my course* ... After a hectic schedule of meetings and consultations Fred prepared to return by way of Singapore where the overseas mission headquarters was now situated. His flight home was booked on the Comet—the first ever commercial jet aeroplane, built by de Havilland Aircraft and which had been in service for just one year. In contrast to today's aircraft it could carry only thirty-seven passengers but flew at the then phenomenal speed of 475 mph. As it landed first at Bangkok to refuel, Fred disembarked for a few moments to take the opportunity of addressing the waiting missionaries who had come to greet him. 'We have pledged ourselves to go forward,' was his challenge but added in a sombre tone, 'but we must expect severe testing.'

With a pilot who had a flying record of over a million miles at the controls in the cockpit, the powerful aircraft roared skyward once more. Fred sat comfortably, glad to be going home. Passing over Calcutta the pilot sent out a reassuring message, 'Climbing on track.' Then there was silence. All contact with the Comet seemed to have been lost. The next day the astonishing news flashed around the world that the much vaunted Comet had been found smashed to pieces lying in a paddy field twenty-two miles from Calcutta. There were no survivors.

Stunned, Christians worldwide could scarcely take in the news. Fred Mitchell, well-loved Home Director of the China Inland Mission, had indeed been climbing on track and had been taken heavenward. It seemed that words written of Enoch long ago were

---

5 My own parents were among the first to settle in Malaysia after 21 years in China.

true also for him: *He was not, for God took him.* Some months later two other Comet aircraft also crashed and it was eventually found that a design defect had led to fatigue cracking in the pressurised cabin.

Such a loss left many grieved and searching for answers. Why had such a valuable man been taken at a time when he was needed most? Dr Martyn Lloyd-Jones, who took the memorial service held for his family, friends and the wider circle of the grieving Mission, on 26 May 1953 had words of consolation as he spoke to the hearts of all who attended: 'There are no accidents in the case of God's children ... God cannot make mistakes. Why? Because he is the Lord—his ways are always perfect.'

8. Praying Johnny: and what happened in Filey

In the grassy and somewhat overgrown graveyard of St James' Church in Warter, a village not far from Pocklington, East Yorkshire, stands an unusual gravestone, commemorating the life of an unusual man. The tribute, though worn with age, can still be read:

> 'Tis not on marble, nor on gilded page
> To print thy worth, thy charity display,
> For chronicles like these may in an age
> Be lost, and in oblivion pass away;
> Eternity itself will best unfold
> The souls by thee led to the heavenly fold.

Who then was this remarkable Yorkshire man, whose life is celebrated in these words? Was he some outstanding preacher, or perhaps a bygone vicar of St James'? The records of John Oxtoby's life tell a far different story.

Little Givendale, a hamlet too small to figure on most maps, was John's birthplace in 1767, a child of farm workers. With little education, the lad grew up with few options other than to become a farm labourer like his father. But John was not without ambition to better himself and tried to save part of his weekly wage for this purpose. At last he had managed to put aside a considerable sum of money—but life gave the youth a bitter blow—he entrusted his savings to someone he had believed would help him, but was robbed of it all. Whether this led to years of abandoned and careless living as one biographer suggests, we are not to know. But certainly at this period of his life he had little thought or concern for God or for any eternal issues.

Not until he was thirty-seven did anything change. Although he did not know it, John Oxtoby was living in significant times in the history of the church of Jesus Christ in England. In 1791 John Wesley had died, but his legacy lived on—a legacy known as the Eighteenth Century Evangelical Revival which saw the birth of Methodism. During the lifetime of men like John and Charles Wesley, George Whitefield, William Grimshaw and many others, vast numbers of men and women were swept into the kingdom of God. But more than this, their preaching had spawned a host of lay preachers who took that same gospel up and down the country and most particularly in areas of Yorkshire.

Such a Methodist lay preacher, nameless in the annals of the records of the Christian church, visited Little Givendale in 1804 and John Oxtoby heard a message that filled him with alarm. According to this preacher, unless John repented of his sins he stood condemned before a holy God. In great distress he hoped the local vicar could help him, but although he offered to pray with John, he could find no suitable prayers in the Book of Common Prayer. Instead he turned to the section marked 'Prayers for the sick'. 'Are you feeling better now, John?' he enquired. 'Not a bit, not a bit,' answered Oxtoby, 'you might as well have poured cold water down my back, mun, as read me them prayers. I want summat different frae that.'

With no one able to help, John's spiritual anguish became yet more acute. Hardly sleeping or eating, he wandered up and down until his friends feared he was losing his reason. But all the time he was praying that God would have mercy on him. And it was a prayer God heard. Another Methodist preacher visited the area just at this time and from his sermon John learnt of a Saviour who had paid the price for sins and was waiting to show him mercy. John Oxtoby's joy at finding the way of forgiveness knew no bounds.

Amazed at what God had done for him, Oxtoby's first instinct was to tell all his friends and neighbours both of their sins and of the mercy of God through the cross of Christ. But their reaction was far from what he expected. Some were angry at such impertinence; others abusive, while some decided the man was mad. But as he walked up and down the streets of Warter, knocking on every door, it became obvious that Johnny, the farm hand from Little Givendale, was a changed man. And gradually, very gradually, doors began to open as he offered to pray with one family after another.

Before many months had passed Warter became a different village. Lives were transformed as the short, thick-set man with a kindly weather-beaten face, hair plastered down his forehead, repeated his message. Now as he walked the streets of Warter, doors flew open. Each family was eager for him to come in and pray for them. If he passed by some home, an anxious householder would peer out the door and shout. 'What have we done wrong that you have missed us out, Johnny?' Before long Oxtoby was known simply as 'Praying Johnny'.

For the next fifteen years Johnny travelled ceaselessly throughout the East Riding of Yorkshire speaking to any he met of Christ and the forgiveness of sins. And all the time he maintained his work as a farm labourer. The effect of his words changed many lives, for these were days when God was working powerfully by his Spirit in many different parts of the country.

Particularly was this true in the rise of a movement called Primitive Methodism. Like Oxtoby himself a few working men, this time from the Potteries, had been powerfully converted and were eager to influence all whom they knew by that same message. Hugh Bourne, a painfully shy farmer's son, William Clowes, a skilled potter from the Wedgewood family, Daniel Shubotham, an infamous waster who earned his living by poaching—these were the men God raised up in a new movement of his Spirit. They had no thought of starting a new denomination, but their enthusiasm and passion was an embarrassment to many Methodists whose ardour had cooled over the years following the deaths of the great eighteenth-century preachers.

Before long John Oxtoby joined them. Having had scant educational opportunities and with little gift for public preaching, it may be surprising to learn that wherever 'Praying Johnny' went his words were amazingly effective. The answer lies in the nickname. John Oxtoby was a man who knew how to plead with God in prayer, and spent long periods on his knees before his Maker. Added to this he had a deep compassion for the souls of his fellow men and women. Approaching a coarse and decadent community, his biographer tells us that 'He looked on the moral waste before him with the tenderest sympathy for the souls of men and cast himself into the midst of such [a community] as one determined to conquer.' And conquer he did by God's grace. Whole towns were as powerfully affected as Warter had been when Oxtoby first started visiting the homes of his neighbours and friends.

Much of his preaching was in the towns of Yorkshire: Hull, Leeds, Halifax, Tadcaster as well as places further north, but perhaps the most memorable account that has survived of Praying Johnny's work is in connection with the town of Filey.

Filey had been notoriously indifferent to the preaching of the Primitive Methodist preachers who had tried in vain to awaken this fishing community to the message of the Christian gospel. Was it worth sending further preachers to this community? Its future hung in the balance. At a Quarterly Association Meeting in Bridlington it was decided to give up any further effort to reach such unresponsive people. John Oxtoby listened in silent dismay. Then someone turned to him, 'What do you think?' he asked. 'Think?' Johnny burst out, 'I think the Lord has a great work to do in Filey and if you will send me, I will live on potatoes and salt and lie on a board if necessary before it shall be given up.' Johnny was sent to Filey.

Packing up his meagre possessions, Johnny set off. 'Where are you going?' someone asked. 'Going? I am going to Filey where the Lord is gannin to revive his work,' came the confident answer. Arriving at a cliff top overlooking the town, Johnny knelt behind a hedge to plead with God to show mercy on the town. How long he knelt there, we do not know. A miller chanced to pass that way some time later and heard strange sounds coming from behind the hedge. He thought it was two men arguing. But it wasn't. It was one man alone with his God. 'Thou munna make a fool o' me,' he was saying. 'I told them at Bridlington thou wast gannin to revive thy work and thou maun dea so or I will never show my face among them agin and then what will the people say about prayin' and believin'?' And as the miller listened in astonishment, this noble man of prayer suddenly leapt to feet with a cry of triumph. 'It is done, Lord; it is done. Filey is taken! Filey is taken!' he shouted. God had given him a secret assurance that his prayer was heard. And Filey was taken.

Entering the town, Oxtoby began to preach in the streets, stopping anyone he could. More and more people began listening with deep concern as Johnny told them that their eternal destiny was at stake. These fishing communities lived lives of imminent danger as their menfolk set off again and again for the fishing grounds. Some would never return, perishing in the icy waters of the North Sea. But with hearts made tender by God's Spirit many at last believed the message that Praying Johnny preached. Memories of that amazing revival of religion still linger in the folklore of Filey even today for the town was indeed 'taken' for the Lord of Hosts.

Johnny's lifespan was swiftly running to its close. With little care for his health or strength, he had given all his energy to preaching and praying, anxious to make up for the earlier wasted years of his life. As the 1820s wore on, it was clear that he was failing. Like the Wesleyan Methodists, the Primitive Methodists also sent their preachers from circuit to circuit, never staying in any one place for more than a year of two. Darlington, Barnsley, Halifax, Tadcaster and Leeds were all privileged with visits from Praying Johnny in this last period of his life, and many are the extraordinary accounts of scenes that accompanied his preaching and of dramatic answers to his prayers. But now with great sorrow everyone could see that Johnny's days of effective preaching were over. It was 1830 and he was sixty-three; with few of his family left, Oxtoby wanted to go to his sister's home in Londesborough to die.

The principles that have governed a person in life will often also reveal themselves in death and so it was with Johnny Oxtoby. Since his conversion in 1804 he had held Jesus Christ as precious above all others in his thought, conversation and lifestyle. 'Tell them,' he whispered to a friend when the end was near, 'that Jesus Christ is present and precious—wonderfully precious to my soul.' In life a deep concern for the souls of others had been his ruling passion and now in death he was still praying for the salvation of those living without a thought of eternity. His last whispered prayer with strength swiftly ebbing, was 'Lord, save souls; do not let them perish.' And as he himself passed from time into eternity his friends could just catch the words, 'Glory … glory … glory.' Well might the words on his gravestone read:

> Eternity itself will best unfold
> The souls led by him to the heavenly fold.

9. Benjamin Ingham: Yorkshire's first apostle

Four young friends—three of them would-be missionaries—were sailing to Georgia in a frail vessel named *The Simmonds*. The year was 1735. All three were destined to be among the most influential men in the long history of the Christian church in England, but not yet. Their names were John and Charles Wesley, both born in Epworth, Lincolnshire and Benjamin Ingham from Ossett in Yorkshire. And an event during this voyage was to be of enormous significance for each of them.

In addition to the eighty or more English passengers on *The Simmonds* there were twenty-six Moravians, earnest Christian believers from Hernhuth in Germany. The journey had been rough with intermittent storms weakening the vessel but throughout the Moravians seemed cheerful and untroubled. Each day they held a service on board and sang their own Moravian hymns. Then one day as they were singing together a ferocious storm erupted—a storm that made all they had experienced so far seem as mere ripples. John Wesley describes what happened:

> In the midst of the psalm wherewith their service began, the sea broke over, split the mainsail in pieces, covered the ship, and poured in between the decks, as if the great deep had already swallowed us up. A terrible screaming began among the English. The

Germans calmly sung on. I asked one of them afterwards, 'Were you not afraid?' He answered, 'I thank God, no.' I asked, 'But were not your women and children afraid?' He replied, mildly, 'No; our women and children are not afraid to die.'

Their calm assurance astonished John Wesley and also had a deep effect on Charles and Benjamin Ingham. These three were deeply religious men, members of the Holy Club in Oxford, devoted to good works and painstaking efforts to win the favour of God. But after this experience in the storm each knew there was a vital element lacking in his spiritual understanding. We read of Ingham:

> The Spirit of the Lord began to convince him of his sin in the ship as they were going to Georgia but he laboured hard to establish his own righteousness ... At length having used all means and finding them ineffectual and in deep distress he looked to Jesus, called on him for mercy and instantly obtained it.

Born in 1712 in a part of Yorkshire where little spiritual light had penetrated, Benjamin had been a serious boy from an early age. As soon as he mastered his alphabet he would read passages of Scripture every night and often found a secret spot where he could pray. At the age of sixteen he gained a place at Queen's College in Oxford, but a shock was awaiting him. He found his contemporaries were facetious and ready to mock anyone with religious convictions. It was not long, however, before he discovered a group of serious young men who regularly met together to study the Scriptures, pray and seek to earn their acceptance with God through prison visiting and other good works. This group were known mockingly by other students as the Holy Club—a name that has stuck.

Ingham kept a private diary during this time that recorded his own efforts to please God. Written in code it has been a hidden document for many long years, but the secret code has comparatively recently been cracked, and now we have a record of his zeal and efforts—one that is truly astonishing. Fasting regularly, spending long hours in prayer each day, Ingham however knew little peace and joy in his religion. How could he be sure he had done enough to please God?

Finishing his studies in 1734, Benjamin Ingham returned to Ossett where his mother still lived and lost no time in gathering his neighbours to his home and explaining the meaning of passages of Scripture. Before long he began classes for the local children and was soon travelling around the area preaching wherever he could gain a hearing. If any were affected by his words he would organise them into small society meetings where they could pray and sing together. Yet for all this, Ingham himself was far from happy and this was the state of things when he suddenly and unexpectedly agreed to join the Wesleys on their mission to Georgia in 1735.

A changed man after that voyage, Ingham found a new freedom and power in his preaching which is not surprising, considering his fresh experience of the grace of God. However, the progress in Georgia among the Indian population was slow particularly as he had to master a difficult language. By 1737 Ingham realised he needed help and decided to return to England to recruit more workers.

Not surprisingly, his first destination on returning home was to head for Yorkshire. But once again God interrupted his plans. Deciding to rein in his horse on Wooley Moor about six miles from Ossett, he chose a vantage point where he could look over the familiar territory of his home town. And we read that as he sat contemplating the scene 'the Spirit of the Lord was poured upon him', baptising him with a new measure of spiritual power and a heart aflame with a desire to preach the gospel. Consequently, he started travelling all over the area, gathering crowds together in chapels, churches and even barns, and wherever he went his preaching was powerfully effective. In fact, he never returned to Georgia. Benjamin Ingham can rightly be called the first apostle of Yorkshire.

These years were ones that have rightly been described as 'the years of God's right hand'. It was evident that a powerful movement of God's Spirit was at work in the land. Both John and Charles Wesley also returned from Georgia, Charles through illness and discouragement in 1736 and John, disillusioned and troubled about his own spiritual condition, early in 1738. May 24 1738 is a day famous in Methodist annals when John attended a Moravian meeting in Fetter Lane and at last received a powerful assurance of his acceptance with God through forgiveness of his sin. Not many days later Charles too found a day when he could truly say 'my chains fell off, my heart was free'.

Meanwhile Benjamin Ingham continued preaching throughout West Yorkshire. An early biographer records: 'In this year 1740 the word of the Lord went on gloriously in Yorkshire.' He continues by giving an impressive list of locations where Ingham had established societies made up of converts from his preaching. These included such places as Dewsbury, Brighouse, Mirfield, Bingley, Bradford, Cleckheaton and many more. Each month Ingham would announce a collective meeting for all these small groups and often two thousand or more converts and enquirers would gather together.

With all this activity taking place news of Benjamin Ingham's preaching soon reached Ledstone Hall, the stately home of Theophilus, Lord Hastings, Earl of Huntingdon which lay not far from Ossett. Surrounded by woodland, the spacious hall was now the home of the Earl's sister, Lady Betty Hastings. Well known in the area for her philanthropic work, Lady Betty was often visited by her four half-sisters, daughters of her father's second marriage following the death of his wife. The Ladies Anne, Frances,

Catherine and Margaret were fascinated by accounts of all that was going on in the area and expressed a wish to meet this Benjamin Ingham. Before long he found himself invited to preach in the Earl's private chapel, Ledsham Church. The sisters listened first out of curiosity, then with interest and soon with increasing concern as Ingham showed them their spiritual need. He was regularly invited to preach whenever they were in the area. Concern soon turned to true heart religion as each of the women became convinced of the truths they heard from Ingham. But with Lady Margaret, the youngest of the four, there was an added dimension as a warm friendship sprang up between Margaret and the twenty-eight-year-old Ingham. They married in 1741 and made their home in the village of Aberford, five miles north of Ledstone Hall.

As converts and societies multiplied under Ingham's preaching and leadership, he made the decision in 1742 to hand over his first sixty Societies to the charge of the Moravians whom he had invited to help him in the work. It was an unfortunate decision because although Ingham and the Wesleys had been powerfully affected by the Moravian Christians, they also discovered that a strand of divisive and false teaching had infiltrated the movement, leading to much dissension. It was called 'the stillness movement' and it maintained that all that anyone who was anxious about spiritual things need do was to 'be still': stop praying, stop attending worship, stop reading the Scriptures and just 'be still' before God.

Although Ingham initially opposed this as an error he later partially adopted the ideas himself, to the vast detriment of his work. Freed from the responsibilities of caring for his many Societies, Ingham continued preaching wherever he had opportunity. As the years passed he became disenchanted with this minority Moravian teaching and sought to undermine it instead and establish his own Societies once more. Once more thousands of men and women flocked to hear him preach, aided by gifted preachers who worked with him. By 1755 further Societies made up of Christian converts had sprung up all over Yorkshire and into Cumbria.

These were embryonic churches, and soon barns and outhouses where people gathered became too small for the burgeoning numbers who wished to be part of an Ingham Society. Permanent premises would have to be built. These became known as Inghamite churches, soon increasing all over Yorkshire, into Lancashire and up into Cumbria. Able preachers grew up among the Societies who either had settled ministries or itinerated among the Inghamite churches.

But for all his many gifts and charisma, Benjamin Ingham was no administrator and seemed to need a model to follow. Having broken away from the Church of England in 1755, he and his Societies were vulnerable to wrong influences. Influenced first by false Moravian teaching, Ingham became caught up by another heresy, described as a 'horrid blast from the north'—a heresy known as Sandemanianism. This emphasis had sprung up from the teachings of John Glas who was a minister of the Church of Scotland and his son-in-law Robert Sandeman. Expelled from the Scottish churches for false teaching these two men propagated their own movement. Their central heresy was to insist that the only thing required of those seeking salvation was to give mental assent to the teachings of Scripture. Emotions accompanying conversion such as sorrow for sin and a warm embrace of the atoning work of Jesus Christ were unnecessary the Sandemanians taught. Saving faith was little more than a mere adherence to a formula.

It is astonishing that Ingham should have embraced this teaching, given his own background of warm spiritual experience and faith. Other divisive Sandemanian ideas were also introduced into the Inghamite churches at the same time. These included foot-washing ceremonies, the holy kiss and the community of goods. Seriously divisive was an insistence on total unanimity for all church decisions—a thing rarely obtainable. Soon prominent leaders broke away, many taking their congregations with them. Members of other churches were scattered to the winds, scarcely knowing where to turn. Some returned to the Church of England, others gave up church attendance altogether. In 1762 William Grimshaw of Haworth reported receiving over one hundred ex-members of Inghamite Societies into his work. Out of almost one hundred churches only thirty remained with Ingham as he struggled to implement some of these new strange ideas.

Gradually Ingham realised what a disaster had hit his life work. The effect on him was grievous. 'I am lost, I am lost,' he would cry out in despair. His sister-in-law, Selina Countess of Huntingdon, wrote to him doing all in her power to lift him from the depths of his gloom. And Ingham was deeply grateful. 'A thousand and a thousand times do I bless and praise my God for the words of comfort and consolation your Ladyship's letters conveyed to my mournful heart, dismayed and overwhelmed as it was by the pressure of my calamities. Righteous art thou, O Lord, and just are the judgements.'

This last statement sets the right note for Benjamin Ingham's last days. He was not tortured by constant despair. Although sorrowing over the past he continued to preach. William Grimshaw could report to the Countess of Huntingdon that he had visited Ingham and found him 'preaching Christ with wonderful success and inexpressible benefit to the souls of many.'

We know little of the final years of Ingham's life. He died in 1772 at the age of sixty, and though he made mistakes of judgement in his ministry we may unhesitatingly declare him one of Yorkshire's truly great preachers. About twenty-five of his chapels lived on, some into the twentieth century and two, Earby Road, Salterforth and Wheatley Lane in Burnley still exist today —a silent monument to his memory.

10. John Wycliffe: father of the English Reformation

John Wycliffe, a young academic studying at Merton College in Oxford, was deeply distressed. Bubonic Plague had broken out in Europe in 1346, sweeping through towns and villages destroying up to sixty percent of the population. The Black Death! And now in 1348 it had begun its devastating passage through England. Rumours from his home village, a few miles from Richmond in Yorkshire told of numerous victims. Were his parents alive or dead? What about the rest of his family? Two thirds of the population of the West Riding of Yorkshire would be wiped out before this cruel plague had run its fearsome course. Eventually it would kill one and a half million out of England's total population of four million. Few of the living remained to bury the dead. Over sixty percent of Londoners were perishing. Anxiously John Wycliffe examined his own armpits, his neck, his groin for signs of lumps or angry black spots, the tell-tale harbinger that spelt near certain death within three days. But John did more than that.

Probably born about 1324, young John Wycliffe had shown early signs of academic brilliance and had arrived in Oxford when he was under sixteen, studying first at Queen's and then at Merton College. Like all young people at that time he had absorbed from the church the teachings of the Papacy, believing that his acceptance with God depended on his good works and his obedience to church dictates. He had listened to services intoned in Latin and seen frescoes on church walls depicting the

Last Judgement with vivid flames of hell devouring those who failed to reach the required standards.

But now, with death staring him in the face, as the Bubonic Plague spread far and wide, John Wycliffe felt waves of panic sweeping over him. How could he be sure of heaven if he died? He must shut himself away with fasting and prayer and seek the forgiveness of God for his sins. We are told, 'This visitation of the Almighty sounded like the trumpet of judgement day in the heart of Wycliffe.' And in those dark days of fear 'he mercy sought and mercy found', through believing on the life and death of Jesus Christ on his behalf for his salvation. This understanding that acceptance with God was not by good works but through Christ was contradictory to the teaching of the Catholic church but became totally foundational to Wycliffe's subsequent thinking and living. It qualifies him to be called the 'Father of the Reformation' almost two hundred years before Martin Luther nailed his ninety-five theses to the church door in Wittenberg on 31 October 1517.

From this time on, Wycliffe began to study the Bible in deadly earnest. For him it was the authoritative message from God himself. Anything and everything taught by the church that contradicted the Scriptures must automatically be in error—and this was the message he began to proclaim fearlessly. The first to feel the onslaught of his brilliant mind were the 'begging friars'. This movement, originated by men like St Francis of Assisi, had become increasingly corrupt, with its friars travelling around teaching false doctrines to the people. As Wycliffe wrote, 'The Friar stuffs the people only too effectually with garbage.' Under the guise of poverty, they were actually enriching themselves by selling absolutions of sin at apparently cheap prices but in reality at exorbitant prices—a con the people readily fell for.

John Wycliffe went further. Not only were the begging friars cheats and hypocrites, but the Papacy itself with its representative in the person of Pope Urban V, had no rights to claim tribute payment from England and its king, Edward III. This humiliating payment had been set up by King John some one hundred and fifty years earlier, but now king and parliament, taught by the writings and pronouncements of Wycliffe, refused to pay. The Papacy threatened to invade England and even excommunicated the King. With the barons threatening to fight back, the arguments continued. At last King Edward sent four delegates, one of whom was John Wycliffe himself, to Bruges to represent England's cause. With the two years of fruitless argument that followed, Wycliffe's attitude to the Pope was hardening. He now spoke of him as 'Anti-Christ, the proud, worldly priest of Rome'.

Despite the failure of the mission, Wycliffe's influence was growing and the King rewarded him by appointing him Rector of Lutterworth in Leicestershire. But he had also made enemies. We read in John Foxe's *Book of Martyrs*, 'The whole glut of monks and begging friars were set in rage or madness which did assail this good man on every side.' John Wycliffe was now in no doubt about the errors and corruption of the Papacy. But pre-eminently his guide and beacon was the Bible. If the teachings of the church contradicted the Scripture they must be exposed and denounced and this John Wycliffe did fearlessly and at personal cost. The Pope condemned him as 'a master of errors', and accused him of 'damnable heresies' ordering his trial and imprisonment in 1377. But Wycliffe had powerful friends, including John of Gaunt, son of King Edward III, and the trial ended in a farce. Step by step this Yorkshire Christian man was leading his country onward in its conflict with the Papacy—a conflict that would culminate a century and a half later when Henry VIII wished to divorce Catherine of Aragon.

Gradually however, Wycliffe also began to lose favour with the English church, especially when his fearless and logical mind took him on to deny the whole doctrine of transubstantiation. How could the bread and wine, held aloft by the priest in the service of the Mass, be transformed into the actual body and blood of

Christ? When Jesus first instituted the simple service of remembrance celebrated in the Communion he was standing before his disciples, his body whole, his blood not yet shed. His meaning was plain. These elements were symbols only of his body and blood. But this conclusion was a step too far for the English church. John Wycliffe was told to be silent on that subject and threatened with imprisonment if he dared repeat such teaching. Even his supporters such as John of Gaunt melted away.

Undeterred Wycliffe appealed to Parliament, proposing sweeping changes in church and monastic life. These would involve the State taking over some of the vast possessions that the church had accumulated by bleeding the peasantry with its crushing demands. This, together with his insistence that transubstantiation was a satanic lie, brought this good man into serious trouble. When the Peasants' Revolt took place in 1381, shaking the nation to its core, the church was quick to lay the blame on John Wycliffe for stirring up the people. Brought to trial once more under the jurisdiction of William Courtenay, Bishop of London, Wycliffe was effectively silenced and banished from Oxford. But he had the last word: 'With whom, do you think you are contending? with an old man on the brink of the grave? No, with truth itself. Truth is stronger than you and it will overcome you.'

And it did. Wycliffe retired to his Lutterworth parish and there he spent the last two years of his life. Although the Bishops intended to silence him, it was at this time that he accomplished his greatest lifework: translating the Bible into English—the language of the people. The only text he had to work with was the Latin Vulgate, the version translated from a variety of Greek and Hebrew documents during the fourth century by Jerome, secretary of Pope Damascus. Quietly and diligently Wycliffe worked with the help of one or two others to give us our first English Bible. Because he had no Hebrew and Greek manuscripts, the translation is often clumsy, sometimes misleading, but a number of expressions present in the King James Version of 1611 are taken straight from Wycliffe's work, expressions such as 'Enter thou into the joy of thy Lord' and some others. Despite the early English spellings, the translation is not difficult to understand. So Genesis 1:1 reads, 'In the bigynnyng God made of nouyt heuene and erthe. Forsothe the erthe was idel and voide, and derknessis weren on the face of depthe.'

John Wycliffe worked ceaselessly although often sick and weary. Time was at a premium for he was nearly sixty and had a great task to finish. Adding to the work of translation, was the fact that all had to be written by hand, for William Caxton's printing press was still nearly a century distant. If possible, he was hated yet more by the ecclesiastical hierarchy for this noble endeavour. A later Archbishop described him as 'this pestilent and most wretched John Wycliffe ... a child or pupil of Antichrist, crowned his wickedness by translating the Scriptures into the mother tongue.' Mercifully, Wycliffe also had many friends willing to labour on the task by copying out the whole or parts of the Scripture to meet the seemingly unquenchable thirst of the people to read the Bible for themselves.

Not only were there willing scribes around him, but also many highly able men already trained in the universities, sometimes called 'Wycliffe's Bible Men'. More popularly they were known as the Lollards. These were men educated for service in the church but thoroughly persuaded of the errors of the Papacy and Catholicism. Up and down the country they travelled carrying portions of Wycliffe's Bible, preaching ceaselessly to the people that acceptance with God did not depend on their good works but on the mercy of God through Jesus Christ. Not surprisingly the clerics hated them even more viciously than they did Wycliffe himself, but undeterred, Wycliffe trained more and more 'Bible Men' and commissioned them to preach everywhere: village greens, barns, public places, wherever they could secure a hearing.

Even in these frail last years, Wycliffe's enemies could not leave him alone, and before long he received a summons to appear before the Pope in Rome. He was willing to go and put the errors of the church before the Papacy itself. But God intervened—he wished his faithful servant to attend a higher court—the court of heaven. A severe stroke made any travel out of the question. Not many days later while attempting to dispense the Communion, he suddenly became paralysed and fell. It was another stroke. Loving hands carried the stricken preacher to his home where he died two days later. It was 31 December 1384. He was about sixty years of age.

Although this heroic Yorkshire man had been removed from the scene of his endeavours, his influence lived on. During the next thirty years or more the evangelical preaching of his followers, the Lollards, was powerfully effective. So great was their influence, bringing men and women to know the truths of Scripture that Wycliffe himself has been called the Morning Star of the Reformation. But with such spiritual achievements among the people the virulent anger of the church broke out in fearful intensity against the Lollards. Many faced the anguish of death at the stake with incredible courage. Wycliffe himself was out of their reach, but there was one thing they could do. They could still condemn him as a heretic. And on 9th December 1427 the order was given to desecrate his grave. His bones were disinterred and publicly burnt, then his ashes were thrown into the River Swift at Lutterworth. Now at last they were rid of him. And indeed it seemed they had won. For the next hundred years truth itself went into hiding. But in 1526, once more in Oxford, light broke out as scholars began secretly reading the New Testament in English, this time translated by William Tyndale. And before long, the candle, lit by John Wycliffe flared into a brightly burning light, as the Reformation broke out in England.

11. Ruth Clark:
a servant girl

A heavy burden rested on Ruth Clark's young shoulders. Her father, a wealthy businessman from Leeds, Yorkshire, had suddenly and inexplicably disappeared. Ruth, who was born in 1741 and the second eldest of nine children, was only ten at the time he went missing. A tenth child was due shortly. Her father had prospered in business and the family enjoyed a comfortable lifestyle; her contemporaries and childhood friends were Isaac and Joseph Milner who would become two of the most erudite and influential men of the century.

But there was one fatal flaw in the family life: Ruth's father was a gambler. He had not learnt from the fearful incident known as the South Sea Bubble of 1720 when shares in the South Sea Company had rocketed and then crashed, bankrupting thousands of investors. And thirty years later he too foolishly invested the whole of his family's wealth in some dicey project—and lost everything. Unable to face the consequences, he walked out of the family home and was never seen again, presumably having committed suicide.

He left his family in dire straits. Ruth's elder sister went into service in some nearby home to support the family and Ruth took on the responsibility of caring for her seven younger siblings while undertaking small spinning jobs at home. Her frail mother never recovered from the shock of what had happened and not long after the birth of her tenth child she too died.

With no welfare system, Ruth soon knew that she too must go into service to earn the money so desperately needed by the family. As a young teenager she found employment as a laundry maid in a wealthy home. Bright, competitive and hard-working, she soon gained a reputation for cheerful efficiency. Always eager to be first to display a full line of washing, she would get up very early on a Monday morning and start scrubbing the clothes while it was still dark. So impressed was her employer that she promoted Ruth to kitchen duties and taught her culinary skills and home management, skills that would be very important in her life.

By the time she was eighteen, Ruth needed a new job. Her reputation for competence was now well known in the area and before long someone recommended the young woman to an Anglican minister who was about to become responsible for a parish in Huddersfield. That might have been all right, but then Ruth heard rumours that her new employer—Henry Venn—was a 'Methodist'. Strange things had been circulating about these new religious enthusiasts who called themselves 'Methodists'. 'What is a Methodist?' Ruth thought in alarm. 'They do nothing but pray and preach,' taunted her friends. But the one who had recommended Ruth to Henry Venn said to the worried girl, 'Go and judge for yourself, Ruth. I predict you will never leave the service of such a master once you try him.' And he was right.

But things were far from plain sailing at first. Ruth found to her dismay that her new master called the household together each morning for an act of worship before the day began. 'What a waste of time!' thought Ruth. To divert her mind, she spent the time counting the number of flowers on the wallpaper. All the household staff were expected to attend Sunday worship—again a real trial to the new mistress of the kitchen in Henry Venn's home. And Ruth had a temper that could flare up at a moment's notice. Again and again Venn would call the irascible young woman to one side and rebuke her for her constant loss of control. But the value and excellence of her work made her position in the kitchens beyond question.

Yet Ruth was not as careless about spiritual issues as Venn thought, and one thing that affected her deeply was the death of Henry's wife, Eling. Henry and Eling had only been married for ten years and her death left him with their five young children to care for. Before she died Eling Venn had shown a special concern for Ruth and spoke seriously to her. 'Make it your first concern, Ruth, to be prepared for death and trifle no longer with your soul,' she warned. 'In what state should I have been in if I had not a Saviour to look to?' Ruth was deeply affected by such words and in the secret of her bedroom cried out to God to have compassion on her and save her soul.

Despite the intensity of his grief Henry Venn was conscious that his young servant girl was indeed seriously concerned about her state before God. Wisely he said little but watched, waited and prayed. On many occasions he still had to rebuke Ruth for her loss of control, but each time this happened the young woman was plunged into despair. But at last a day came when Ruth was listening to a sermon in Henry Venn's Huddersfield church. She understood at last that Jesus Christ saves broken, needy, despairing men and women by his death on the cross. Tears ran down her cheeks as she realised both the depth of her sinfulness and the strength of her pride that had hindered her for so long. But they were also tears of joy as she knew at last that her sins had been forgiven for Christ's sake.

Ruth did not overcome her boisterous temper and caustic tongue all at once, but gradually, very gradually she was changing as the power of the grace of Christ gave her strength to control these traits of nature. And her work, if possible, improved. Or at least she did not complain when extra pressure was laid on her. On one occasion when John Wesley and his entourage came to stay in the Huddersfield vicarage Ruth found herself with eighteen extra sheets to wash by hand in her small washtub. Locking herself in the laundry room she scrubbed steadily until the task was done, only to return to the kitchen to prepare dinner for many extra guests.

It soon became clear that Henry Venn was exhausted. The duties of a bustling town parish together with the care of his five young children had sapped his strength. With a degree of relief, he accepted a change: a small country parish in the village of Yelling, not far from Cambridge. Would Ruth go with him? She was a Yorkshire girl and all her siblings and their families were in Yorkshire. But the words of the one who had recommended Ruth to work for Venn proved true. 'You will never leave the service of such a master once you try him,' he had predicted, and Ruth gladly accompanied Venn and his family to Yelling.

Once again, Ruth kept her new kitchen in a spotless condition. Her brass pans were buffed up till they shone like mirrors and her floors were scrubbed clean every day. So when Venn suggested that he would like to invite the villagers into the kitchen every evening for a service of worship, she must have gulped hard as she thought of all the mud they would tread in on their boots after a hard day of toil in the fields. Bravely she commented, 'What does it signify if the people do but get good for their souls?' Yet all the same, the moment the last villager left she could be seen with a little knife scraping the mud off the stools and rewashing her floors. And Ruth loved the village folk. She would often visit them in their homes if they were sick, taking with her small gifts of food from the kitchen.

As news of the ministry at Yelling spread, many students from Cambridge would walk the twelve miles to listen to Venn's preaching or to ask him questions. And students need feeding. So Ruth would find that she had to provide many extra dinners on a Sunday for those who had tramped from a considerable distance to attend the services.

Nor had Ruth Clark forgotten her own family. She wrote regular letters to her brothers and sisters and included notes of kindly spiritual advice to their children. But with a typical human touch she always enclosed a little gift in with her letters to her nieces and nephews, to sweeten her words. When one of her brothers died his four young children were in danger of being taken into the workhouse—the worst of all scenarios in those days. Ruth sent regular maintenance for the family out of her own wages, leaving little for her own old age.

Busy years passed as Henry Venn's work in Yelling expanded, but with grief Ruth could not help noticing how her master was ageing. The end came quite quickly for Venn died in 1797 at the age of seventy-two, and Ruth felt the loss as much as any of his family. 'Oh Ma'am,' she said to one of his daughters, 'when one gets to heaven, to see the Saviour, that will be first, but then next to see my dear and honoured master, what a joy and delight!'

Ruth herself had another ten years to live and Eling Elliot, one of Venn's daughters, invited her to stay in Brighton where she and her family were living. Gladly Ruth accepted, and even though she no longer had charge of the kitchen she still had many a piece of homely advice to pass on to Eling about economy and kitchen management!

A sad accident cut Ruth's own life short, as a runaway horse and cart crashed into her before she had a chance to move out of the way. The injuries she sustained broke her health and at the age of sixty-seven her own desire to 'see the Lord' was fulfilled. The end was not easy for Ruth. 'It is hard work to die,' she confessed to one of the Venn sisters who had called to see her, yet added quickly, 'but I have a hope which is able to support me.'

'Have you any doubts?' asked her visitor gently.

'Oh no, none!' she replied. 'He (Christ) that has loved me all my life will not forsake me now.' And nor did he. Ruth died in May 1807 and was buried in the same grave as Henry Venn himself—a mark of the honour in which the family held her.

12. William Wilberforce: setting the captives free

A small sensitive-looking man, only five foot three in height, is sitting in the two-seater coach crushed by a man of enormous bulk. The small man is William Wilberforce, his friend is Isaac Milner. Both are Yorkshire men. These two are setting off together for a Grand Tour of the Continent, a highly fashionable pastime for the well-to-do in the eighteenth century. In another coach various female relatives of Wilberforce, his mother, sister and cousins will be travelling.

Charming, witty and highly intelligent, young Wilberforce, now aged twenty-five, had just been elected as MP for the whole of Yorkshire in 1784, after only four years as a representative for Hull, the city of his birth. A great achievement it certainly was, but the campaign had been highly exhausting. So now he would have opportunity to relax—or so he thought.

Isaac Milner had other thoughts. He was William's senior by nine years and had been an usher at Hull Grammar School when young William was a pupil. Isaac's older brother Joseph Milner was headmaster at the time and had secured his brother this place. Both men, sons of a Leeds weaver, possessed an extraordinary intellect. Patronised by his brother, Isaac had secured a place at Queen's College Cambridge and went on to become a brilliant mathematician, scientist and inventor. After only four years at university his tutors could only write 'incomparable' to describe his attainments. But this man of so high an intellect and so immense a bulk had another side to him: he was an evangelical Christian.

And now he had William Wilberforce's spiritual good in his sights. Patiently he waited his opportunity, entering into engaging conversation on many other topics. It came when Wilberforce had to return to London for urgent parliamentary duties. Leaving the ladies in the party behind, he and Milner set off. On the way back Wilberforce casually referred to a book he had seen called *The Rise and Progress of Religion in the Soul* by Philip Doddridge. Yes, Milner agreed, it is a remarkable book. And together the two men began to study its closely written pages. The impression on Wilberforce was profound. It set him thinking as never before and banished his somewhat derogatory opinion of men and women who take their Christian profession seriously.

So much had Wilberforce enjoyed Isaac Milner's company that following the parliamentary session he invited him to return with him to rejoin the ladies. This time Milner brought with him a Greek New Testament and during their period on the Continent the two men studied the book ceaselessly—to such an extent that the ladies started complaining of neglect.

Although now convinced intellectually of the truth of the Scriptures, Wilberforce did not at first allow his understanding to affect his way of life. But by the time they were due to return in October 1785 he had undergone a powerful revolution in his thinking and spiritual convictions. 'Oh the deep guilt and black ingratitude of my past life,' he exclaimed, 'when eternal happiness was within my grasp.' William Wilberforce was a changed man. From now on he lived with one purpose in view: to serve his God by striving with all his power to improve society and relieve the distresses of the needy.

Born into a rich merchant family in Hull, East Yorkshire, in 1759, young William had had a tough beginning to life. Small and delicate, it was touch and go as to whether this baby would survive. Infant mortality was still very high, but survive he did and was soon showing evidence of an unusual intelligence with exceptional powers of speech. At the age of seven he was sent to Hull Grammar School and Isaac Milner, then acting as an usher at the school, tells of how they used to put this diminutive boy up on a table and ask him to read aloud as an example to the other boys.

Two years later when William was only nine, his father died. His mother was also seriously ill at the time, whether from the same infection or from stress and grief, we do not know. It was decided to send William to the home of his uncle and aunt in Wimbledon. Here the child was loved and cared for and he became extremely fond of his Uncle William and Aunt Hannah. They took the boy to hear the preaching of some of the outstanding Methodist preachers of the day, men like George Whitefield and John Newton, the one-time slave trader. The quality and sincerity of his relatives' beliefs impressed William deeply and with all his own childish fervour he responded to the preaching he heard. But after about two years his mother caught a whisper that her child was 'becoming a Methodist'. She was furious. Without delay she travelled to Wimbledon and spoke angrily to her brother and sister-in-law and took William back home with her. From then on she did all in her power to crush any religious interest William may have imbibed. And she succeeded. William was heartbroken at first, though with the resilience of a child he soon put aside his previous inclinations, becoming pleasure-orientated and light-hearted.

At seventeen young Wilberforce began his university education at St John's College, Cambridge—a period when he quickly imbibed the somewhat dissolute ways of his fellow students. A deep purse gave him licence for little serious study and a lot of 'fun'. But by the time he graduated at the age of twenty he had developed an interest in politics and enjoyed watching proceedings in the visitors' gallery in the House of Commons. Here too he met William Pitt and the two forged a warm friendship. Wilberforce's chance came at the General Election of 1780 when with the advantage of cash to buy influence and his family connections, he secured the position of MP for Hull as an Independent, sweeping to a large majority.

Steadily the new MP for Hull gained first respect and then admiration largely on account of his astonishing eloquence. As James Boswell vividly reported: 'I saw what seemed a mere shrimp (a reference to his height), but as I listened he grew and grew until the shrimp became a whale.' Four years later the loss of the War of American Independence meant that Parliament was dissolved and the country was plunged into another election. This time Wilberforce's ambitions soared as he contested and won the seat for the whole of Yorkshire. From now on he would be an important and influential Member of Parliament. And it was at this time that he travelled to the Continent with Isaac Milner—a trip that would change his life forever.

With his conversion to biblical Christianity, William Wilberforce's goals and aspirations in life were dramatically changed. And it did not take long for his contemporaries to notice. Foremost of these was a group of friends who would collectively become known as the Clapham Sect, men who lived on or near Clapham Common. Now swallowed up in Greater London, Clapham Common conjures up the image of a bustling and noisy railway junction but in the 1780s and 90s it was far different. A haven of quiet green peacefulness, the Common provided a home for tired and overworked business men and politicians, lying only three miles from London.

Thomas Clarkson was prominent among the Clapham friends. A tall red-headed academic, Clarkson had written a prize-winning essay which he had entitled 'Is it right to make a slave of others against their will?' Shocked to the core by the discoveries he had made of the sufferings of the African peoples during his study, he was utterly dedicated to do all in his power to alleviate such horrors. Could this politician, William Wilberforce, so radically changed, do anything to help? In January 1787 Clarkson tentatively asked for an interview with Wilberforce at his home in New Palace Yard, situated next to Westminster Abbey. In his hand he carried a copy of his essay. Unknown to Clarkson, Wilberforce had already given the subject much thought, but he merely assured Clarkson that the matter was 'near his heart', and that he would read the essay to learn more.

Two months later Clarkson invited Wilberforce to a dinner function together with other prominent figures. Armed with the information he had read in Clarkson's essay, the young politician, now twenty-seven, was full of zeal for the cause. By October 1787 Wilberforce began preparing seriously to take up the issue and work for the abolition of the slave trade. But this was no easy task. Huge vested interests were at stake coupled with eighty percent of British overseas trade, most notably with the sugar plantations of Jamaica. Towns like Bristol had been built up and flourished on the trade. By the 1780s British traders had carried over 325,000 slaves across the Atlantic to work in the sugar plantations. Any diminution of the trade would bring colossal problems and no politician wanted to be seen to be working against the public interest.

In 1789, frail from a recent illness, Wilberforce prepared to give his first major speech in the House of Commons for the abolition of the slave trade. With natural eloquence this five foot three giant of a man spoke with persuasive passion for three and a half hours, approaching the subject from eight different angles, each one challenging in its own right. But if his reasoning was powerful and disturbing, his enemies were vicious in their opposition, and in the end Wilberforce felt he could not press for a vote. It was a grave disappointment. So began the long and relentless Parliamentary campaign on behalf of the benighted slaves of West Africa.

Although as a prominent MP Wilberforce was the front runner in this long race, he was by no means alone. Backing him up and providing him with vital statistics were other men of astonishing ability and earnest Christian character. Thomas Clarkson has already been mentioned. Henry Thornton was the foremost of the Clapham Sect, providing much of the finance for its endeavours. Perhaps the most unsung hero of the anti-slave trade campaign was Zachary Macaulay, father of the great English historian Thomas Babington Macaulay. With a mind of remarkable brilliance Macaulay was an encyclopaedia of facts and figures. He undertook the role of supplying Wilberforce with information for his many speeches. 'Look it up in Macaulay,' he would say if he had any doubts.

Many were the speeches Wilberforce delivered on behalf of the slaves, but again and again his pleas fell to the ground unheeded. England had too much to lose and humanitarian concerns weighed light in the balances against prosperity and trade. But there was one issue where Wilberforce prevailed with astonishing speed. As a bachelor, now thirty-seven years of age, he met the beautiful Barbara Spooner who was only twenty. Wilberforce fell passionately in love. And he brooked no delays. Complaining that this charming girl was filling his thoughts by day and his dreams at night, he proposed to Barbara just one week after first meeting her. She accepted and they were married five weeks later.

But the 1790s were difficult years for these courageous men advocating the abolition of the slave trade and other reforms. Largely this was due to the French Revolution with the Storming of the Bastille in 1789 and the following fearful executions of men and women in positions of power and influence. What if that should happen in Britain? Parliament was frankly scared of the fury that might be unleashed if the slave trade were abolished. Again and again Wilberforce's graphic pleas were outvoted by the House of Commons or the House of Lords.

At last, as the new century unfolded, the tide gradually began to turn. By this time Wilberforce and his wife Barbara had moved into part of a large house on Clapham Common—a house with several wings and thirty-two bedrooms—known as Battersea Rise. Here friends could mingle and confer and the library became their 'conference centre' in the truest sense where each step of their campaigns could be plotted.

Several commercial reasons have been suggested for the changes of attitudes, one being the overproduction of sugar which caused demand to shrink. A sizeable number of Irish members of Parliament now had seats in the House changing the balance of power. These were representatives of a race that had often been crushed and were sensitive to the sufferings of others. But pre-eminently a new wave of spiritual revival was touching the consciences of the people. God himself was at work. As men and women became concerned for their state before God, hearts were softened over the distresses of their fellow men and women.

At last came a great day—perhaps the greatest day of William Wilberforce's whole life: 23 February 1807. When yet another bill to abolish the slave trade in the British empire came to the vote Parliament passed it by 283 to 16. The applause was thunderous. Tears poured down Wilberforce's face as Parliament rose as one man to congratulate him with resounding cheers for the success of his endeavour after seventeen long years. Yes, it was a shared endeavour but this small man with his slightly humped back and poor health rightfully deserves the honour accorded to him.

But if Wilberforce, now forty-seven years of age, thought that the fight was over he was mistaken. He and the other abolitionists came up against huge vested interests, together with the refusal of other countries such as France, Spain and Portugal, to implement the new ban on the slave trade. Outburst of malicious abuse from ship owners filled the press together with character smears against Wilberforce and chiefly Zachary Macaulay whom angry ex-slave traders quickly identified as their hidden foe. Macaulay was given the thankless task of tracking down ships that were breaking the law, and discovered some English traders sailing under bogus flags and others cruelly dumping their cargoes of slaves into the sea if they feared imminent capture.

Many other humanitarian concerns such as the Society for the Suppression of Vice and Catholic Emancipation occupied Wilberforce's attention, together with the responsibility of bringing up his family. Somewhat disorganised as a character, his days were hectic and the steady stream of visitors who wished to consult him relentless. From 1812 onwards with health deteriorating he began a slow withdrawal from the incessant demands of political life. He sold his home Battersea Rise on Clapham Common moving to a quieter area of Kensington.

Passionate though he was for social reform in a wide variety of spheres of national life, Wilberforce had a deep and urgent concern for the spiritual good of individuals who were his friends or part of his life. Cheerful, yet profoundly serious, he was anxious for the spiritual state of his own sons and wrote long and searching letters to each one begging him to examine his soul before God. To his mother whose early antagonism against his faith had been so marked, he wrote:

> May you, my dearest mother, learn of your own demerits as a sinner and of the mercy and love of God who holds out promises of pardon and acceptance to all penitent believers in Christ.

Even when this big-hearted small man was silent, his very presence was a challenge in itself. On one occasion he visited a friend, a seriously ill man—a peer in the House of Lords. Filled with pity, Wilberforce said nothing as he sat by the bed. Just at that moment another friend entered the room and asked the invalid how he was doing. 'Well enough,' replied the peer, 'considering Wilberforce is sitting here telling me I am going to hell.' Clearly Wilberforce's presence alone was sufficient challenge in itself.

Nevertheless, this big-hearted man yearned to see earth-moving changes—and above all the total abolition of slavery itself. Although he introduced bills to this end, in his heart he felt that the nation had not the appetite for this further battle. As the years passed Wilberforce himself had not the strength to continue the endeavour. In fact, few could conceive of such a possibility ever becoming a reality and most of the Clapham Sect gradually moved away from the Common, leaving only the Macaulays with their family of eight and the Thorntons living there. But it was Zachary Macaulay with a determined one-track mind who continued to fight doggedly for the cause.

In 1825 Wilberforce, now far from well, resigned from his position as MP. But with Macaulay's incessant labours other men of influence gradually joined the cause and Wilberforce's parliamentary mantle fell on Thomas Fowell Buxton who continued to plead for the abolition of slavery. Then came the vital Reform Act of 1832 with fifty-six smaller boroughs disenfranchised and the addition of sixty-seven new constituencies. The balance of power had changed again. At last in 1833 a further bill for the Abolition of Slavery in the British Dominions came before the House. The motion teetered on the edge as various amendments were demanded, and Macaulay kept the dying Wilberforce in touch with every development. Then on 26 July the Bill passed its second reading. When Wilberforce heard the news he said simply, 'Thank God I have lived to witness this day.' Three days later he died. A handsome bust was erected in Westminster Abbey to commemorate the astonishing achievements of this great little man.

Perhaps the best accolade comes from the pen of his own son Henry Wilberforce who described his father in these last days of life as one who was 'looking forward to future happiness but seems more like a person in the actual enjoyment of a heaven within'.

13. John Fawcett: binding hearts together

A twelve-year-old boy is standing by an open grave in Lidget Green, a village now swallowed up in West Bradford, Yorkshire. A coffin carrying the body of his father, Steven Fawcett, is about to be lowered slowly into the grave. Beside the boy stands his blind grandfather, weeping. 'Let me just touch my son's coffin,' he begs. Kindly, the blind old man is led forward, touches the coffin, then covers his tear-stained face with his hands. It was a scene young John Fawcett never forgot.

Born in 1740 in Lidget Green, John was a member of a large family. The times were hard. And now, with his father gone, who would provide for his widowed mother and the family? At the age of twelve, John would be expected to work to help provide some income. It was these circumstances and his grandfather's helpless grief that turned John's mind to the One who cares for the fatherless and widows as he began to look to God to help in this time of extremity. But another issue was also weighing on the youth's mind. What about his father's eternal destiny? John didn't know. He had loved his father dearly but also understood enough Scripture to recognise the vital importance of this question. Night and day it was all he could think about until one night he had an unusual dream and in this dream he was given an inner assurance that his fears for his father were groundless. All was well with him. Later in life John would admit that apart from that dream he feared he would have never ceased grieving over his father.

More than this, however, these circumstances awoke in John Fawcett a strong desire to be assured of his own spiritual state in case death took him unprepared. A clever boy, he began reading voraciously any book that would develop his understanding of spiritual issues. And one book above all others stood out: John Bunyan's *The Pilgrim's Progress*. Written almost a century earlier this spiritual classic touched John deeply. As he read of Christian fleeing from the City of Destruction, his own longings for spiritual certainty increased until like Bunyan's pilgrim he too found that the burden of his sin had gone when he came to the Cross. 'I saw One, as I thought in my mind, hang bleeding on the tree and the very sight of him made my burden fall off my back,' declares Christian.

Whenever he could snatch a moment John could now be found avidly reading some of the great classics of the Christian faith. But time was at a premium for the boy was serving an apprenticeship which kept him fully occupied from six in the morning until eight at night. With candles bought from his earnings flickering at his bedside John would steal time from the night hours to read, particularly the Bible itself. In order to keep himself awake he would resort to the expedient of tying a weight to his foot or fastening one hand to the bedpost! Although such measures gradually told on his health, they demonstrate young John Fawcett's earnest desire to seek after God.

It is not surprising to learn that this ardent-minded youth came to the attention of some of the great men of the eighteenth century revival whose preaching was being used to awaken the nation to its need of true religion. When John or Charles Wesley or George Whitefield came to Leeds or Bradford or any of the surrounding towns John Fawcett would be amongst the crowds who flocked to hear them preach.

But above all it was the ministry of William Grimshaw in Haworth which drew Fawcett again and again, walking the thirty or more miles each Sunday to be able to attend his dynamic preaching. This he did for over two years, but very gradually, as Fawcett met and listened to some of the leading Dissenters of the time, his opinions regarding baptism and church government changed. To Grimshaw's intense disappointment Fawcett no longer attended his preaching but walked a couple of hundred yards further on down the road in Haworth to listen to the preaching of James Hartley, one of Grimshaw's own converts, who had also become a Dissenter and opened a Baptist Chapel within sound of the Haworth parish church bell.

When Fawcett was nineteen, two changes took place. First he fell in love and married and secondly he gave up his long weekly treks to Haworth and joined the Baptist Church in Bradford—both excellent developments. For the first time he was able to become part of a local church and soon began to show deep interest and affection towards other church members, a trait of character which would mark his future career. Before long his pastor encouraged him to attempt to preach. Overcome by nerves his first endeavour was a disaster, but with loving support his next effort was a great improvement. Before long Fawcett was preaching around and not surprisingly a church whose pastor had recently moved away invited the twenty-five-year-old John to become its pastor.

Hebden Bridge, west of Bradford, lies in a valley not far from Haworth, a place John must have known well from his weekly walks to hear Grimshaw preach. It derives its name from the old bridge that spans the fast flowing Hebden River, fed by streams gushing down from the Pennines that tower above the old market town. As a result, the town has suffered from repeated flooding, but Wainsgate Baptist Chapel to which Fawcett was invited stands on a windswept hillside above the old town. Built in 1750 the chapel was poorly constructed and it soon became evident that the walls were not high enough. To correct this fault, the floors were excavated to the depth of eighteen inches during the ministry of its first pastor, Richard Smith. But this only solved one problem to create another: the building became cold and damp.

When John Fawcett and his young family arrived at Wainsgate he found a small and somewhat impoverished congregation. Mainly farm workers and labourers, they were only able to offer him a meagre £25 a year as a stipend. This was in days when an average working man might receive £40. Fortunately, John was able to augment his income by picking up his pen and starting to write, publishing his first work—a book of poetry—two years later. And his preaching too began to attract men and women from further afield who climbed the steep hill to Wainsgate Chapel, Sunday by Sunday. Among his hearers was John Sutcliff, later to become pastor of Olney Baptist Church and whose influence on William Carey, regarded as the Father of Modern Missions, was profound. Under Fawcett's ministry John Sutcliff was baptised and encouraged to study for the ministry at Bristol Baptist Academy.

Word of Fawcett's ministry at Wainsgate began to spread and on one occasion he was invited to preach in Southwark, London, to the congregation of the renowned theologian Dr John Gill, pastor of Carter Lane Baptist Church. Although his preaching was well received, he did not expect to hear anything more. But in 1772 the unexpected happened. A letter arrived inviting him to succeed as pastor the great Dr Gill himself who had recently died. Fawcett had been at Wainsgate Chapel for seven years and had grown to love his people dearly. But Carter Lane! This was the church which would one day invite the young C. H. Spurgeon to be its pastor, under whose ministry it eventually became the great Metropolitan Tabernacle, attracting over five thousand worshippers each week.

Many urged Fawcett to accept the invitation—it was an amazing opportunity. Wainsgate was still unable to offer an adequate stipend to enable John to support his growing family; the building was damp which did not improve his health, and above all, a London pulpit would give him an extended usefulness as a preacher. The struggle was profound. At last Fawcett decided he must wrench himself away from the people he had grown to love so dearly, away from his native Yorkshire, away from his family roots and go to London.

So began the painful task of selling up items of furniture that he could not take with him and hardest of all some of those precious books that he had collected over the years. With heavy heart he attended a farewell service, and then the wagon containing all his belongings was loaded up. His wife and children clambered aboard. Slowly the heavy wagon rumbled off, with all his Wainsgate people following him weeping.

But no! He couldn't do it. John Fawcett knew at that moment that he could never leave these people whom he loved, however glittering the invitation might be. Dismounting, he told his grieving congregation that he was not going to leave them. Nor did he, staying with that same congregation for the rest of his life.

In reference to these unique circumstances John Fawcett wrote his most memorable hymn, one often sung at funerals and times of parting:

> Blest be the tie that binds
> our hearts in Christian love;
> the fellowship of kindred minds
> is like to that above.

> We share our mutual woes,
> our mutual burdens bear;
> and often for each other flows
> the sympathising tear.

When for a while we part,
this thought will soothe our pain,
that we shall still be joined in heart
and hope to meet again.

This glorious hope revives
our courage by the way,
while each in expectation lives
longs to see the day.

From sorrow, toil and pain,
and sin we shall be free;
and perfect love and friendship reign
through all eternity.

The rest of John Fawcett's life must be quickly told. For a further five years he continued to minister at Wainsgate Chapel. The numbers grew (but sadly his stipend did not). At last the damp and cramped conditions were seriously undermining John's health. For some time, he had been urging his people to build a chapel in Hebden Bridge itself to replace the severe and grey building on the windswept hillside above the town. There they could worship in a warmer and roomier chapel. But Yorkshire folk can be very stubborn and many were unwilling to move. At last a compromise was reached: Fawcett and half the congregation had a chapel built in the valley below. It was to be known as Ebenezer Chapel, appropriately using the biblical word meaning 'Hitherto has the Lord helped us'. Some of the congregation remained at Wainscote. The old chapel still stands today and is used for concerts and other functions, but reportedly it is still cold. The new chapel is now renamed Hope Baptist Church.

John Fawcett's ministry was not limited to his preaching. Many books on various aspects of theology flowed from his ready pen as well as more than a hundred and fifty hymns. It is said that he wrote the hymns to accompany his sermons. Although the standard of verse is not exceptional, three or four have found a place in modern hymnals, with the lines already quoted taking pride of place. Added to this he started his own training academy for young men who felt a call to the ministry from God. His first students gathered in his home, but when the numbers increased he hired nearby premises and eventually moved the burgeoning Academy to Halifax. It is not surprising, therefore that in 1792 John Fawcett received an invitation to become the new President of Bristol Baptist Academy.

Now fifty-two and in poor health, John Fawcett felt that the upheaval and responsibility would be too much for him. He declined the invitation. It shows however how much this Yorkshire lad from a poor background had attained in his life through dedication to his calling and devotion to his God. Despite failing strength and the loss of his wife in 1810, Fawcett continued preaching in Hebden Bridge whenever he was able, and in 1811 he was awarded an honorary doctorate by an American university for his exceptional contribution both to literature and to the Christian ministry.

For his last sermon, just a year before his death, John Fawcett took for his text Nahum 1:7, *The Lord is good, a stronghold in the day of trouble*, for so he had found him to be. And in July 1817 at the age of seventy-seven this faithful servant of Jesus Christ was taken from the trials and sorrows of this life to that better land where tears and pain are gone forever.

14. Robert Arthington: the generous recluse

Few men and women are remembered principally for what they accomplished after their death—certainly none in these pages—apart that is from Robert Arthington.

Born in Hunslet Lane, Leeds in May 1823, Robert was the son of wealthy parents, Robert and Maria Arthington. He was their only boy and with his three sisters, the family were Quakers, belonging to the local Society of Friends—his father a leading member of the Society. Robert Arthington, senior, had made his colossal wealth in the brewery industry, so the children had a comfortable home and upbringing.

These were the days of the burgeoning railway system as it was developing in England. The Stockton and Darlington line, the first commercial railway had been opened in 1825 when Robert was two and we can well imagine the boy's fascination with trains as new lines were steadily opening during his childhood. But the highlight must have been when the Hunslet Lane Railway line opened on his very doorstep when he was seventeen. It is not surprising therefore that Robert Arthington showed much interest in the commercial development of rail in later life.

Little is known of Robert's early years. He studied at Cambridge and showed excellent academic ability and scientific acumen, but the most significant development in his life was the remarkable change—even the split that took place in the family—as his mother, two of his sisters and Robert himself left the Quaker movement and joined the local Baptist church. We are not told how this happened but clearly there must have been a convincing spiritual dimension to effect such a change in the family. It could well be that Robert came in touch with young men of strong Christian persuasion while studying at Cambridge, was converted and then was used to influence his mother and sisters.

Robert was baptised by immersion and joined South Parade Baptist Church in 1848 when he was twenty-five. We read that those who first built South Parade Baptist Church in 1825 were 'men of profound piety and wide charity, and the impress of their lives still remains in the deep spiritual life that has always characterised the Church'. Even today the church, now meeting in various parts of Leeds, boasts a membership of five hundred.

Two other things profoundly affected Robert Arthington's life at this point. Remembering that his father's vast wealth was made through the brewery industry, we are surprised to learn that at this time Robert, senior, became convicted of the devastating effects of alcohol, particularly among the poverty-stricken neighbourhoods around Hunslet Lane. He closed down his business and lived in strict temperance for the rest of his life although he did not sell the business. Robert followed his father's example as a teetotaller in this respect.

The other influence which would mark out Robert's entire future life was his strong allegiance to the Premillennial view of the Second Coming of Jesus Christ. Based on verses in Revelation 20 which speak, possibly figuratively like much of the rest of the book, Premillennialism teaches that at a certain moment in world history Satan will be bound and cast into a pit for a literal period of a thousand years. During this time Christ and his people will reign on earth. When that Millennial reign is over Satan will be released from his bonds, will gather his army and the great Battle of Armageddon will take place. Christ will win, and the victory will be followed by the ultimate destruction of Satan together with the Final Judgement of mankind. This teaching, coupled with various indications foretold by Christ—words that pointed to the near fulfilment of these events, was widely held by many good and godly men and still is today.

But one element of Christ's teaching on this subject, gleaned from his words to his disciples who had asked him for signs of the End of the Age, affected Robert's whole future in a profound way. In Matthew 24:14, Jesus told his disciples, *This gospel of the kingdom will be proclaimed throughout the whole world as a testimony to all nations, and then the end will come.* So when the entire world has had an opportunity to hear the gospel of Jesus Christ, then he will return and Satan will be bound for ever. From that moment on Robert Arthington lived with one single aim: to spread that gospel and so to hasten the coming of Christ—a grand aim but it led to some strange consequences in this man's life.

Both of Robert's parents died in 1864 within months of each other, leaving him the enormous legacy of £200,000 which in today's values would be over £8,000,000. What would he do with such wealth? With considerable business acumen, Robert had been keeping his eyes on the rapidly increasing railway systems both across Victorian England and even more importantly in America. Now he invested heavily in that enterprise. As a result, his wealth became phenomenal. What did he do with it?

First, in 1868 he bought a plot of land in Headingley Lane, Leeds and had a handsome stone property built for himself: again, a wise investment of money. But from this point on Robert Arthington trod a strange and to most a totally inexplicable path. As a bachelor he felt he needed little and so occupied only one room in this house. He restricted his weekly expenditure to a half crown (a half crown, or two shillings and sixpence in old money and in today's values about £6). How did he manage that? we may ask in astonishment. Heating and lighting costs were no problem to Arthington, he did without. In fact, he said it was quite adequate to speak with his friends as they sat together in the dark. He had no bed but slept in a chair at night, covered only by his coat, a coat which he wore each day for the next seventeen years. His meals were basic. The neighbours who did not know the motivation for Robert's strange lifestyle called him the 'Headingley Miser'.

How wrong they were! Here was possibly the most generous man in the world. First he got to know some of the students who came to Leeds and when they were in financial difficulties he helped them out. But far more importantly as far as Robert was concerned was the worldwide spread of the gospel in order to hasten Christ's return. As a member of a Baptist church his first major gifts were to the Baptist Missionary Society. Founded in Kettering in 1792 by a small group of pastors with a deep concern for the spread of the gospel, the Society had commissioned William Carey to go to India, promising to support him as much as they were able.

By the 1870s the mission was spreading worldwide and particularly into Africa. An important expansion into the Congo region was being planned towards this goal when Arthington donated £1000—about £46,000 today. But shipping was also needed to penetrate the more inland areas along the River Zaire, now the Congo River. So in 1880 he financed a ship belonging to the explorer George Grenfell. a ship called *Peace*, with a gift of £4,000. Grenfell, who planned to penetrate eastwards from the coast, would eventually reach as far as the equator. He established his headquarters near Leopoldville, calling the place Arthington. Supplementing this gift with a further £2,000 in 1882, Robert was anxious that by means of the ship the Baptist Missionary Society should eventually meet up with the areas where the

London Missionary Society was working. This would form a corridor of evangelism right across Africa reaching many previously unknown people groups with the gospel.

The number of missionary causes Arthington supported during the remainder of his life is too long to enumerate—a closely written article which can be read on the internet runs to over four thousand words listing all the endeavours he assisted across the globe. The needs of India did not escape his attention. He established his own Arthington Aborigines Mission in 1889 in order to evangelise the tribal people in the northeast of the country. Translations of the Gospels and the Acts of the Apostles were of vital importance in his view for these could penetrate where missionaries were unable to gain entry.

During Arthington's lifetime he gave money to most of the important missionary societies, an amount totalling some £23,000 —a sum which in today's values would be £1,377,470. Nor did he give without extensive research and specific projects in mind, an enterprise which must have occupied most of his waking hours. And always his motivation was the same: to reach the peoples of the world with the gospel. It can be claimed that this recluse living in one room in Headingley Lane was the impetus behind much of the missionary endeavour and advance during that great age of the expansion of foreign missions in the late nineteenth century.

Added to this Arthington also had eyes for local requirements. The medical condition of women and children around him in Leeds moved this generous man with deep compassion as he donated £20,000 towards the establishment of a hospital to relieve such needs. And so Robert Arthington's strange life drew to a close. But the astonishing good that he accomplished in his lifetime, is dwarfed by the good he did in his legacy after death.

Robert Arthington died on 9th December 1900. We presume that he now had a bed to lie on instead of his chair covered with a coat. And in his dying he asked the friend visiting him in his lonely single room to read to him from Christ's Sermon on the Mount and from Psalm 72. As he listened to moving words from the Psalm such as *Blessed be his glorious name forever; may the whole earth be filled with his glory,* he said simply, 'Yes, it is all there—all.' This had been his life's ambition, to see the whole earth filled with the glory of Christ. His gravestone bears the words: 'Robert Arthington, His life and wealth was devoted to the spread of the Gospel among the Heathen.'

Arthington's name lives on as a byword for generosity; his lifestyle was eccentric and not one to be imitated, but his heart for the spread of the gospel is exemplary and humbling. Found among his papers after his death was a letter from a missionary who wrote, 'Were I in England again, I would gladly live in one room, make the floor my bed, a box my chair, another my table, rather than the heathen should perish for the lack of knowledge of Jesus Christ.' This noble aspiration may well be the pattern Arthington followed.

Robert Arthington had prepared his will a few months before he died, making generous provision for his twenty-one first cousins with £111,000 to be shared equally among them, amounting to over six million pounds in today's values. But it represented only ten percent of his available funds. The rest was to be divided between the Baptist Missionary Society, the London Missionary Society and translation work on the Scriptures. Truly here was a man whom God entrusted with riches and who used his stewardship to spread the gospel of Jesus Christ worldwide in an astonishing way.

15.Ezekiel Rogers: God's exile

If you ever want an idyllic spot for a wedding reception you could hardly do better than Rowley in Yorkshire. Represented by a small dot on the map, Rowley lies some ten miles from Hull and not far from Little Weighton. Tranquil pastureland surrounds the old church of St Peter's and Rowley Manor itself, now a luxurious hotel, stands where once the old vicarage had stood. It is approached by a tree-lined glade and surrounded by sweeping lawns. But where, you may well ask, is the village itself? The answer? In New England, America.

In the story of Ezekiel Rogers we find the explanation of this unlikely circumstance. The days were growing harder for the congregation that met week after week at St Peters, drawn not only from the local community but from many surrounding areas. Born in Dedham, Essex, in 1590, their pastor Ezekiel Rogers was the son of Richard Rogers, a gifted and eloquent preacher. The boy grew to maturity, sitting regularly under his father's preaching, and not surprisingly, he too wished to enter the ministry. Completing his university training, he responded to a vacancy at Rowley in Yorkshire and began his ministry there. With much of his father's eloquence and gift, Ezekiel's preaching stirred the village and the congregation soon grew. Week by week their new vicar pleaded with his people to repent of their sins and find the forgiveness of God. Many responded to his preaching and were able to speak of God's gift of new spiritual life.

Then a dreadful realisation dawned on Ezekiel Rogers. He himself was a stranger to the very truths he was teaching. He was just repeating what he had heard his father say. Who could help him? There seemed only one solution. He would saddle his horse and ride the two hundred miles back to Dedham to consult his cousin John Rogers who had taken over the church following Richard Roger's death. Arriving in Dedham as the morning service was in progress, Ezekiel slipped in at the back unnoticed. The sermon he heard was transforming and answered all his questions. No doubt he stayed to talk to his cousin, but soon returned to Rowley with a glad heart. If his ministry was effective before it was now doubly so, as men and women travelled to Rowley from a wide area.

But these were the days when King Charles I and his henchman Archbishop Laud were striving to crush Puritanism and bring all the churches back to a High Church position. The screw was gradually tightening and in 1636 all churches were required by law to comply with certain requirements. These were ones with which Ezekiel Rogers fundamentally disagreed. He now had no alternative: conform or relinquish his living. He did the latter. If he wished to continue his ministry he had no option but to emigrate to the New World, where he would have liberty to preach in accordance with Scripture and his conscience. Calling himself 'God's poor exile', Ezekiel began packing up his home.

'If you are going, we are going too,' his people said. And so they did. One morning in 1638 the village was bustling with activity as the people packed up all their belongings: clothing, furniture, kitchen utensils, farm implements, books, as much as they could cram into the waiting wagons. With the crack of whips the wagons trundled off on their ten-mile trek to Hull. There a small chartered ship called the *St John* was awaiting them. Slowly they boarded, whole families together, children and even newborn babies. So the Rowley congregation left their village home for ever and embarked on a three-month journey to New England.

At last the *St John* cast anchor in Massachusetts Bay. Wearily the Rowley congregation disembarked and soon moved on to land allocated to them in the north of the country. Here they rebuilt their homes and church, gradually settling down. And what better name could they call their new village but Rowley, a reminder of their far distant Yorkshire home and one that still figures on maps today.

Ezekiel Rogers continued to minister to his Rowley congregation for the next twenty-two years. He died at the age of seventy in 1660, exclaiming to another pastor shortly before he died, 'I thank God that I am near home. Oh what a weight of glory is awaiting us, God's poor exiles.'

16. Joseph Milner: when Hull became 'a garden of the Lord'

The boy was frail from his early years. Although healthy enough when he was born in 1744, a serious bout of measles seemed to leave a permanent effect on Joseph Milner. For the next eight years his life often hung in the balance, and each childhood illness left a permanent effect on his overall health. Asthma was a constant problem, making Joseph unable to join in the normal activities so enjoyed by others of his age. But instead the boy shut himself up in some secret place and read book after book. And he had another big advantage—his schoolmaster.

A kindly man, the Rev. Mr Moore, noticed the child reading material well beyond his age, and began to take an active interest in him. He soon discovered that the boy's memory was phenomenal. It seemed there was no verse of Scripture in either the Old or New Testaments, when quoted to him, that he could not turn to immediately. As Joseph grew older his schoolmaster even called on him to help him out when explaining Greek or Latin authors to his other pupils.

But Joseph's parents were poor, his father struggling to support his family through his work in the wool industry in Leeds. But he understood his boy and on one occasion even brought home a Greek book for his boy—instead of the Sunday joint he set out to

buy! He could not afford both, he said! Moore knew however that
if Joseph survived to adulthood he would have no chance of
earning a living in any form of physical work. The only possibility
would be through some academic work. So the kindly
schoolmaster determined to help young Joseph attend university
—it was clear that his parents could not fund such a possibility.

Everywhere he went Joseph's schoolmaster spoke of the little
genius until many well placed locals were prepared to help the boy
gain a place at university when he was old enough. And eventually
through the help of these friends he secured a coveted place at
Catharine Hall in Cambridge. Sadly, his kindly schoolmaster died
soon after Joseph's first year. With the loss of his main benefactor
he was not able to carry on at Catharine Hall beyond obtaining
his degree as he had hoped. This was a blow for Milner who freely
admits that at this time he was 'worldly-minded and greedy of
literary fame'.

The only possibility now appeared to be to train for the church,
but not long after starting on this option together with teaching
at a school near Tadcaster, Milner spotted an advertisement for
the position of headmaster at Hull Grammar School—then a
small and struggling institution. Applying for the job, he obtained
it and soon after was also given a position as a 'lecturer' at Holy
Trinity Church in Hull. This appointment allowed him to preach
at a mid-week service and also meant that he could continue his
theological studies.

With his gifted mind and skill in teaching others, Joseph
Milner's appointment as headmaster of Hull Grammar School
soon boosted the reputation of the school as it became crowded
with hopeful pupils. But Joseph was troubled. His own future
might be secure but what about his younger brother Isaac, still
only ten years old? With an equally brilliant mind, Isaac had
received none of the advantages that Joseph had enjoyed and even
at so young an age had left school and was presently employed as

a weaver in a Leeds wool mill. Now in a position to help, Joseph invited Isaac to join him in Hull as an usher at the school and later he would become a mentor to the younger boys. Isaac Milner could never speak highly enough of his brother's kindness in rescuing him in this way and opening up an astonishing career for him.

Joseph Milner's popularity in Hull was soaring. All the aldermen and officials of the town spoke highly of him, and his afternoon lectures at Holy Trinity Church were packed. Now in his mid-twenties he appeared to have reached the heights of popularity. Yet Milner was conscious of a deep inner discontent. Yes, he was an earnest and zealous preacher, yes, he knew all the biblical teachings but although everything he said was orthodox, even moving for his hearers, he later admitted, 'I preached myself and not Jesus Christ'. It was hard to conceive of anyone in a position to challenge or help him.

But God's ways are often strange, and that he should choose two relatively uneducated men to change the whole course of Milner's thinking is not what we might expect.

Throughout the last forty years God had been at work up and down the country in a remarkable way and Yorkshire was no exception. The inclusion in these accounts of the lives of men like John Nelson, Benjamin Ingham, William Grimshaw and others is evidence of this. And to meet the crying demand for more preachers Selina Countess of Huntingdon had opened a training college in Trevecca (now spelt Trefeca) in South Wales during 1768. This was designed to prepare young men who had no university credentials to their name to travel the country preaching wherever they could gain opportunity. And in 1770, two Trevecca preachers came to Hull.

Dr Joseph Milner may well have been critical at first, but it soon became evident that these two zealous young men were preaching with unusual power and effect. And the people flocked to hear them. Joseph himself listened to their preaching and was deeply affected. Erudite as he was, he discovered a dimension of spiritual life that was totally new to him and aware of his own personal spiritual need he warmly embraced the message they brought. Writing to a friend in London, Joseph could declare how grateful he was for Selina sending her students to Hull for by their message he had secured 'a saving interest in Christ'. It changed his whole life, not only outwardly for all to see but in his whole inner personality and preaching.

But the cost was high, for many of the grandees of Hull who had so loudly proclaimed Milner's virtues, first tried to undermine him and then shunned any service at which he was preaching. Yet he carried on his way steadfastly and still the crowds flocked to hear him. The effect on Hull was astonishing. The city has been described as 'a garden of the Lord' during this period. New places of worship sprang up everywhere and on prayer meeting nights there was the phenomenal sight of thousands of men and women running along the streets in order to secure a seat in some church gathering.

And what of his brother Isaac? In this same year of 1770, Joseph was in a financial position to send his brother to Queen's College, Cambridge where he excelled intellectually, becoming a senior wrangler, mathematician, a member of the Royal Society and an inventor. Of these two Yorkshire brothers, Isaac may have the greater claim to fame, but both had enormous influence on the society of the day. William Wilberforce had been a pupil at Hull Grammar School at that very time and spoke of the Milner brothers in the highest terms. Isaac shared his brother's intense spiritual convictions. As we have seen Isaac's friendship with Wilberforce led to the latter's conversion and on to the incalculable benefits brought to society through Wilberforce's unswerving determination to see the abolition of the slave trade.

For many years Joseph Milner combined his duties at Hull Grammar School, with the charge of a church in North Ferriby, a village on the foreshore of the Humber estuary. He also wrote extensively, his most important work *A History of the Church of Christ*, which would eventually extend to five volumes. The last two of these were actually written by Isaac after Joseph's death, who re-edited the whole in 1810. But as we have seen Joseph's health was not good and repeated bouts of fever undermined his constitution. Holy Trinity Church which had earlier rejected Milner's evangelicalism was now itself much influenced by the power of the gospel in Hull. Too late, Joseph was appointed to the living of this church in October 1797. But he had only a few more weeks to live, and died on 15 November of that same year.

In his will Milner wrote moving words which demonstrate the depth of his spiritual convictions and his hope of the glory to come.

> I thank the Lord Jesus my Lord that he has shown me the way of full salvation through his obedience unto death, even the death of the cross … Hence only I expect to find God to be my God though all eternity. If I have been enabled to perform any [deeds] that are good, though they are imperfect indeed and stained, what is good in them is the Lord's and I shall be glad to give him the glory of it.

17. Miles Coverdale: the first English Bible

The world had grown very dark for Miles Coverdale, John Rogers and many others. Their friend, the highly admired translator of the Bible into English, William Tyndale, was dead. But not from natural causes. His enemies had got him at last.

With a burning passion to give the English peoples the Bible in their own language, Tyndale had been forced to live in exile on the Continent for much of his life. Here he could be moderately safe as he laboured to translate the Scriptures from the original Greek and Hebrew languages into English. Such an activity was considered heresy by the church of his day, who held that the priesthood alone had the right to read and interpret Scripture. By 1526, Tyndale's first translation of the New Testament into English was ready and printed. Smuggled into England hidden in bales of merchandise, it was widely circulated, passed surreptitiously from hand to hand.

And back in Cambridge a young Augustinian friar named Miles Coverdale began to read the English Bible for the first time. Born in Yorkshire in 1488, some say near York, others suggest Richmond, Coverdale was deeply devout. It was however the influence of Robert Barnes, an Augustinian prior and eventually a martyr for his faith, who opened Coverdale's understanding to the truth of what he was reading. His life was transformed by the power of Christ. Described as 'a young man of friendly and upright nature and very gentle spirit', Miles Coverdale left the Augustinians and joined Tyndale in exile and gave his whole endeavour to working with him as he began the enormous toil of revising his New Testament translation and reworking the first five books of the Old Testament, known as the Pentateuch. By 1529 these too were circulating in England.

But now in 1536 Tyndale was dead—at little more than forty years of age. A supposed friend had betrayed him. Thrown into a dank dungeon with few possessions, this fine man was subject to cruel examinations and eventually after sixteen months accused of heresy, taken to Vilvorde, strangled to death and then burnt at the stake. Noble in his life and noble in death, William Tyndale's dying prayer, 'Lord, open the King of England's eyes' was amazingly answered, an answer in which Miles Coverdale played a vital part.

After his imprisonment Tyndale's rooms were ransacked and his many papers and books destroyed. After all, it was argued, a heretic does not deserve to have any memory of him retained. But someone, it is thought to have been John Rogers, got there first and rescued much of Tyndale's work on the Old Testament that he had already accomplished. This included his work on Jonah and many of the historical books of the Old Testament.

What could be done to complete the translation of the Old Testament? The Bible is a whole, and all the books are needed for an understanding of its message. It is here that Miles Coverdale made his gigantic contribution to the Bible we can so readily read today. Not gifted like Tyndale in a mastery of Hebrew and Greek, he was not intimidated. Instead, during the period of Tyndale's imprisonment, he gathered as many translations of the Psalms and the remaining books of the Old Testament as he was able: the German, the Dutch and the Swiss, together with Wycliffe's work.

Toiling assiduously, he rendered these Scriptures into English and oversaw the printing of the whole Bible for the first time.

Some of Coverdale's work suffers as he did not know the original languages, but many of his translations are beautiful, surviving even into the 1611 Authorised Version. His work on the Psalms is particularly moving: *The heavens declare the glory of God*, was his rendering of Psalm 19:1 and *O God, thou art my God, early will I seek thee, my soul thirsteth for thee,* is his evocative translation of Psalm 63:1. In 1535, the year before Tyndale's death and while he was still in prison, the whole Bible in English was circulating clandestinely. Whether Tyndale knew it or not, we cannot say.

Half of the Old Testament, from Job to Malachi, excluding the book of Jonah, was Miles Coverdale's work, and for good measure, most of the Apocrypha as well. But he was not alone. Aided by John Rogers, an accomplished scholar who would later become the first martyr of at least two hundred and eighty-two other men, women and young people cruelly put to death in Mary I's reign, the Bible was printed and attractively produced with about one hundred and fifty illustrations—a remarkable achievement.

Coverdale's purpose for printing this, the very first complete Bible in the English language, is set out clearly in an introductory letter to the reader written in the quaint idiom of the day: 'Go to now, most dear reader, and sit thee down at the Lord's feet and read his words and take them into thine heart … Thou shalt find sweetness therein and spy wondrous things to thy understanding.'

But it was still illegal to possess a Bible and it could bring imprisonment and even death on any discovered reading it. The answer, however, to Tyndale's dying prayer for Henry VIII was not long delayed. Two years later John Rogers edited all the material in Coverdale's Bible, made up almost entirely of the work of Tyndale and Coverdale. He arranged for 1,500 copies to be reprinted. His aim was to present the volume to the men surrounding the king and through them eventually to the king himself, urging Henry to license the Bible for distribution to every parish church in the country. It was a bold endeavour and Rogers was wise as well as daring. He knew that if the names of William Tyndale or Miles Coverdale appeared in the volume it might well be doomed from the outset. Instead the preface stated that it had been 'purely translated into English by Thomas Matthew'—a pseudonym probably coined by using the names of two of the early disciples. Dedicated to Henry VIII himself, the Thomas Matthew Bible won the day and Henry gave it his royal licence. It was 1537, less than a year since Tyndale's martyrdom. Before long 9,000 were needed to cover every parish church in the country.

Miles Coverdale, confident now of freedom from the danger of hostile clergy, returned to England. In 1539 Thomas Cromwell, the King's chief minister, put him in charge of a modest revision of the Bible. This revision largely included improvements to his own work but left Tyndale's virtually untouched except for the removal of a word or two here and there which would cause offence to the brittle-minded clergy of the day. And so was born The Great Bible, named because of its large pages, measuring fourteen inches by nine—a Bible intended for public reading. Copies were chained to every parish church pulpit in the land—all authorised again by King Henry himself.

Sadly, with a temperament as volatile as Henry's, the political and religious situation over which he dominated changed yet again in 1540. Thomas Cromwell, chief promoter of Reformation values, fell from favour and was executed without trial in 1540. Miles Coverdale felt it was expedient to leave English shores, and with his newly married Scottish wife, Elizabeth, fled to the Continent once more. The king, in poor health and short tempered, was erratic. Executions on religious grounds multiplied, including that of Coverdale's early mentor Robert Barnes. Even Queen Catherine Parr only narrowly escaped. These were hard days for those who loved the truths newly discovered in Bibles translated by Tyndale and Coverdale.

But in 1546 King Henry VIII died and his young son Edward, only nine years of age, came to the throne. An earnest Christian boy, Edward and his supporters pushed forward the Reformation in England. Miles Coverdale returned to England after almost eight years of exile and for the brief years of Edward's reign fulfilled a role of great usefulness as Bishop of Exeter and highly popular preacher. But with young Edward's death before his sixteenth birthday, the crown passed to Mary, Henry's daughter by his first wife, Katherine of Aragon. The situation changed dramatically as Mary tried to crush the effects of the Reformation in England. Good men, many being Coverdale's friends, perished at the stake including, tragically, his fellow worker John Rogers leaving a wife and eleven children, one a baby in arms.

Coverdale was in grave danger. It seemed the fires were already heating up to burn this good man. Imprisoned briefly, he was released however, by an intervention from the King of Denmark, protesting Coverdale's innocence. Mary gave permission for his release and he fled to the Continent once more. Here he would remain, a wanderer from one place to another, serving his God wherever he had opportunity until after Mary I's death in 1558. In 1559 he returned once more to his homeland. Now seventy years of age, Miles Coverdale lived out the last eleven years of his life honourably serving the church wherever he had opportunity. With voice and faculties failing, requests for him to preach were still insistent. At last in January 1569 two men had to carry him into the pulpit and according to a contemporary who was present, 'God was (so) with his spirit to strengthen him that he made his last and best and most godly sermon that he ever did in all his life.' A few days later this upright son of Yorkshire died. We do well to honour him.

18. William Grimshaw: a mighty evangelist

If ever Yorkshire was revolutionised through the work of a powerful gospel preacher, it was when William Grimshaw came to a little-known rugged Pennine village called Haworth in 1742. With fewer than a dozen communicants attending the parish church of St Michael's and All Angels, Grimshaw lived to witness a time when thousands streamed up the steep hill to the church each Sunday, some on foot, some on horseback or even some by carriage if they could afford it.

Over two hundred years after Grimshaw's death, Ted Hughes, one of England's former poet laureates who was brought up in nearby Heptonstall, was amazed at the continuing effect of the preaching upon the whole area. Although no friend of Christianity, Hughes could write in 1993:

> To a degree he changed the very landscape. His heavenly fire … shattered the terrain into biblical landmarks; quarries burst open like craters, and chapels—the bedrock transfigured—materialised, standing in them. To judge by the shock-waves which could still be felt well into this century (the 20th), he struck the whole region like a planet …

But things were far different when young Grimshaw undertook his first parish charge in Todmorden, near Halifax. Born in September 1708 in Brindle, not far from Preston, and ordained in 1732, the young man was a heavy drinker, with a passion for little else except fishing, hunting and socialising. The would-be cleric had scant concern for the souls of the people—and Todmorden suited his lifestyle admirably. He became nothing more than a typical eighteenth-century worldly cleric, his highest resolution being to avoid entering the pulpit drunk, while his parish duties were just a source of income and occupied as little time as possible.

With a flair for bizarre methods of discipline in his parish, the story has survived of the day Grimshaw dealt with a young man who had made a girl pregnant but refused to marry her, ridiculing her publicly instead. Fired with indignation, Grimshaw dressed up as the devil, donning a large and ugly mask complete with horns. Hiding in the shadows on a path the young man always took on his way home from work, Grimshaw leapt out at him with a roar. As an iron grip tightened on his shoulder, the young man was convinced that the devil himself had come to escort him to hell for his sins. Desperately afraid, he promised to honour his obligations to the girl.

Cut off from the main streams of social life, Grimshaw knew nothing of the preaching of John and Charles Wesley and George Whitefield that was gripping many parts of the nation at that time. But God had his own means of reaching this man whom he intended to use so powerfully in future days. When a young mother in the parish came to him in distress after the sudden 'cot death' of her infant daughter, he found himself quite unable to help her. 'Put away all gloomy thoughts and go into merry company,' he suggested. It didn't work. But his final piece of advice to the bereaved couple became one which would be a goad to his own soul: 'To despair of the mercy of God would be the worst thing of all.'

From that moment a new seriousness marked the young curate as he himself earnestly searched for that same mercy. He began to keep a ledger. At the end of each day he wrote down all his sins and shortcoming on one page and on the opposite page all his acceptable deeds and prayers. Perhaps his good deeds would balance out the sins, he thought hopefully. But they did not. Nothing brought him peace of conscience. The death in 1739 of his wife Sarah at only twenty-nine, left William with two small children and brought him to the brink of despair in his search for the mercy of God. 'My friends!' he cried out in the middle of a service of worship, 'we are all in a damnable state and I scarcely know how we are to get out of it.'

But there was a way out, and early in 1742 Grimshaw discovered that way through the pages of a book by the great Puritan theologian, Dr John Owen. Divinely and strangely brought to his attention by some unexpected flashes of light, he picked it up off a table in a friend's house. Glancing at the contents page Grimshaw knew immediately that he must read this book. Entitled 'Justification by Faith', he discovered in its pages the answer to his greatest need. Despite all his efforts he had found himself helpless to meet the demands of a righteous God. Now he discovered that the answer lay not in his own standards being acceptable, but in the righteousness of Christ, won for him by the cross. With untold relief he could exclaim:

> I was now willing to renounce myself, every degree of fancied merit and ability and to embrace Christ only for my all in all. O what light and comfort did I now enjoy in my own soul, and what a taste of the pardoning love of God.

Released from the burden of his guilt, Grimshaw had one pressing desire—to preach that message of deliverance to others. And what better time for a fresh start? Remarrying, he responded to an invitation to Haworth, some nine miles north of

Todmorden, and moved there in May 1742 with his new bride, Elizabeth, and his two children. Haworth, now a Mecca for Brontë enthusiasts, could then be described by John Newton as 'a barren wilderness' where the people had 'little more sense of religion than their cattle.'.

Grimshaw was undeterred. Even though he could only count on twelve regular communicants when he started, his fiery preaching soon drew hundreds from a wide area. Like John Bunyan a century earlier, Grimshaw's early preaching centred mainly on the broken law of God and his righteous anger against sin. Someone who heard him reported that 'He frequently rolled like thunder, but mingled tears like the Saviour's over Jerusalem with his severity.'

Despite the enthusiastic response to his preaching, Grimshaw himself still lacked a full assurance of his own salvation, often passing through times when all his new-found joys forsook him as he found himself tossed about by fierce temptation and doubt. But on 2 September 1744 God favoured him with a remarkable disclosure of his love, giving him a vivid sight, almost vision-like in its clarity, of the wounds that Jesus bore for his sin. From that moment, as a friend later reported, 'he was instantly filled with a joyful sense of his interest in Christ'. Grimshaw rarely spoke of this experience, but never again would he doubt his salvation.

With that new assurance came an added dimension to his ministry as he began to preach the gospel of Christ in all its saving power. And during the following eighteen months at least a hundred and twenty were converted. As often happens in the early months of a spiritual awakening, there were many expressions of heightened emotions among his hearers. But Grimshaw discouraged such phenomenon knowing how easily Satan can counterfeit it, so bringing discredit on the gospel. And for many years the work of conversion carried on steadily and powerfully.

Although Grimshaw was at first highly suspicious of the Wesley brothers and of the fledgling 'Methodist' movement, his misgivings were expelled after he met first Charles and then John and experienced a warm affinity with them. From 1747 onwards Grimshaw could rightly be called a 'Methodist' himself, a term initially used to describe men and women within the Anglican church touched by the new breath of spiritual life affecting areas of the country. Now he began fearlessly to follow Wesley's example of preaching beyond the bounds of his own parish, in fact wherever he could gather a 'congregation', whether in a barn, cottage or the open-air. Persecution inevitably followed, but as John Wesley wrote: 'Mr Grimshaw was ready to go to prison or death for Christ's sake.'

'William Grimshaw used his body with less compassion than a merciful man would use his beast,' commented Henry Venn, as he thought of the preacher's tireless endeavours to reach vast areas of the north of England with the message of the gospel. His ceaseless activity, preaching sometimes thirty times a week, led to the development of the 'Great Haworth Round' as it was called, that amazing preaching circuit which could find Grimshaw as far north of Haworth as Hartlepool, or as far south as Sheffield and Chester.

Despite the extent of his travels, Grimshaw would always be back in Haworth each Sunday. He commented that he knew each of his parishioners personally, adding 'I will speak to everyone under my care concerning his soul. If you will not come and hear, you shall hear me at home, and (in broad Yorkshire) if yer perish, yer will perish 'wi' t' sound o' t' gospel i' yer lugs.' He would not lose a single opportunity to speak of the life-transforming gospel to the people. Meeting an old woman on the moors one day he asked whether she had ever heard a gospel sermon. No, she had not. 'Well you shall hear one now,' was his reply, as he exhorted her there and then to repentance and faith.

The change in the whole area was astonishing. 'What has God wrought in the midst of these rough mountains,' exclaimed John Wesley when he visited Haworth in 1761. On occasions six thousand or more would cram into the expansive Haworth churchyard to hear one of the Wesleys, Whitefield or Grimshaw himself preach. Lives broken by drink, immorality and laziness were healed, homes were transformed. And the effect of his ministry was not merely transitory. When James Everett decided to write a biography of Grimshaw in the following century, he discovered evidences of his influence everywhere. Even sixty years after Grimshaw's death Everett could exclaim, 'He seems to meet us at every point, like a sword turning every way to guard the way of the tree of life.'

William Grimshaw died well. His life motto had been words of the apostle Paul from Philippians 1:21, *For to me to live is Christ and to die is gain*, a truth he had demonstrated in his living: and now in his dying. He had often encouraged his people to meditate much on death in order to be ready whenever it should strike. 'Today is your living day,' he would say, 'tomorrow may be your dying day.' Despite his own hardy physique, he anticipated an early death, 'I expect my stay on earth will be but short,' he wrote, 'and will endeavour to make the best of a short life, and so devote my soul to God as not to go creeping to heaven at the last.'

Nor did he. When yet another epidemic of typhus fever swept through the village in March 1763, Grimshaw succumbed to the infection. With his health already undermined by his ceaseless labours, he knew he was dying. The way he died could be called a sermon in itself. To a friend who visited him, he declared: 'My last enemy is come ... but I am not afraid. No! No! blessed be God, my hope is sure and I am in his hands.' And to Henry Venn from nearby Huddersfield, he whispered despite a burning fever, 'I am as happy as I can be on earth and as sure of glory as if I were in it.' After just two weeks of intense suffering, he said to his housekeeper, 'I have nothing to do but to step out of bed into heaven. I have my foot on the threshold already.' And he had, for he died later that day, 7 April 1763.

Deep grief swept over Haworth for Grimshaw was only fifty-four and deeply loved. Thousands attended his funeral, singing and weeping as they carried his coffin the nine miles to Luddenden where his first wife Sarah had been buried. The service was conducted by Henry Venn who preached on Grimshaw's life motto of Philippians 1:21, words also engraved on his coffin at Grimshaw's request. Venn's words rang out clearly across the wooded valley as thousands stood listening: 'Witness, ye moors and mountains, how often he was in perils by the way, whilst carrying the glad tidings of salvation to some poor company of cottagers, who, but for his instruction, had died as ignorant of Christ as they were born!'

Today he is all but forgotten by the thousands who visit Haworth reliving the sad stories of the Brontë sisters, but one writer has made an interesting assessment: 'The whole epic of the Brontë family cannot be separated from the gospel. Had there been no Wesley, the fire had not kindled. Had there been no Grimshaw, there would have been no fierce tale of *Wuthering Heights*.'[6]

An even better accolade is found in the book of Daniel where we read: *They ... that turn many to righteousness, shall shine as the stars forever and ever*, and surely we must count William Grimshaw of Haworth, evangelist of Yorkshire and regions far beyond, as among that number and honour his memory.

---

[6] G E Harrison, Haworth Parsonage, A Study of the Wesleys and the Brontës, London: Epworth Press, 1937.

19:William Scoresby: when God interrupts

To be the son of one of the most successful whalers of all time, an Arctic explorer and the inventor of the barrel Crow's Nest is surely accolade enough for William Scoresby Junior, who shared his father's adventures, to merit a place in any book about worthy characters of the great county of Yorkshire—but there is more to his story, much more.

Born in Cropton, near Pickering in 1789, William seldom saw his father during the first eleven years of life, for William Senior was usually away on his long voyages to the Arctic waters in search of whales. A valuable commodity at the time, these monsters of the sea were mercilessly hunted largely for their blubber—a vital source of oil for lamps and heating before it was replaced by petroleum. Whale meat and bones were also highly prized.

Cutting his way through pack ice, dangers on every hand, William's father braved the wild Arctic weather. But one day before setting off he invited his eleven-year-old boy to join him on board his ship *Dundee* to look round the ship. So intrigued was young William that he was loathe to leave when the ship was ready to sail. In an impulsive moment his father decided to take his son with him and a dangerous journey it proved all through the bitter winter months. But the boy was captivated and joined his father and crew each winter after that, continuing his education in the summer months, and later attending Edinburgh University when not at sea.

When William was thirteen he became officially apprenticed to his father, and so rapid was his progress that he became First Mate of the ship when only sixteen and captain at twenty-one when his father started a new business partnership.

But whaling was not young William's only expertise. He had the mind and skill of a scientist and an inventor. His work on magnetism was groundbreaking as was his mapping of the east coast of Greenland and important findings regarding the temperatures of the Arctic waters below the ice. William was later to record his discoveries by publishing parts of his journals in a book entitled, *An Account of the Arctic Regions*. Many explorers and scientists have performed great feats and made important contributions to our knowledge of the world, but William Scoresby finds a place in our record for a discovery yet more noble and life changing.

Here was a man on the brink of greatness—here was a religious man who believed in prayer and the truth of the Scriptures, but here was a deeply dissatisfied man. And not only that, in 1816 after twenty-five years at sea, a series of near disasters seemed to follow Scoresby one after the other. Not only was his catch of whales poor, his ship *The Esk* struck an iceberg and began to sink. With water rushing in, Scoresby had no alternative but to try and save his crew by ordering them to erect tents on the ice so they could escape the sinking ship. Meanwhile for fifty hours he and his men struggled to bail out their ship and eventually *The Esk* was cut free, but the event left Scoresby deeply sobered and he could only acknowledge God's amazing deliverance.

The next couple of voyages were also singularly unsuccessful and soon this intrepid whaler and explorer began to realise that success alone could never satisfy. Returning home, William attended the ministry of a new clergyman in the area, a man by the name of Holloway, and was touched by all that he heard. Asking to see him privately, Scoresby was encouraged when his new friend assured him that 'God was designing my eternal salvation, and that the work of his Spirit was begun'. But it was not long after this that he received a letter telling him that his brother-in-law to whom he had lent the colossal sum of £1,537 3s 5d had gone bankrupt. This was the majority of William's own resources, and in a moment left him also in poverty—the trigger that made this gifted whaler, scientist and explorer seek the wealth that could never be taken away. Kneeling down, he records, 'I poured out my soul before God with an energy and submission I had never done before—Take away my wealth—all that I have—but give me your grace and blessing. Let my heart and will be forever devoted to you and your will be done.'

Despite the setbacks of 1816, William Scoresby continued whaling for the next seven years, but now his life priorities were far different. He cared for his men in a new way and held services on board for them. And though diffident at first, he even began to address them himself on matters of spiritual concern. During the summer months he gave himself to the study of the Bible and in 1823 left the life of whaling and entered the Christian ministry, serving first at a small church near Bridlington. Many sorrows surrounded his life including the loss of his first wife, Mary Lockwood, and both his sons before they reached manhood. Life was hard in many ways, but now he knew of the sustaining grace of God in such trials. After his remarriage to Elizabeth Fiztgerald, a young Irish woman, six years later, Scoresby moved to Liverpool and then to Exeter. In 1838, when Scoresby was almost fifty he was appointed as vicar of St Peter's in Bradford. And during these years he needed every spiritual resource to cope with the situation he discovered in that city. As we have seen in our glance at Titus Salt's life, the circumstances in Bradford were dire at that time with poverty, filth and crime on every hand. Even the Arctic storms seemed preferable to the 'incessant, laborious and painful' situations that Scoresby faced. Preaching regularly to almost three thousand people, the toll on his health was great and also that of his second wife, Elizabeth. And after nineteen years of marriage, she too died. Broken in health Scoresby eventually resigned from his Bradford charge in 1847 but not before his work had brought lasting improvements in the city, socially, educationally and spiritually.

His last years were spent in Torquay, where he married for the third time—a girl of twenty-one named Georgina—and very happy those last seven years of his life proved to be. He continued ministry as an assistant to a local vicar and also with his scientific work, both lecturing and travelling. At last, in March 1857 at the age of sixty-seven this noble son of Yorkshire, exchanged earth for heaven—for that better country where all sorrows are gone forever.

20. Richard Conyers: Rector of Helmsley

The picturesque village of Lastingham in the North Yorkshire Dales was once known as Læstingau and first appears in the history books in the seventh century when King Ethelwald of Deira (651-c.655) founded a monastery there for his own burial. But we may associate another name with Lastingham for it was the birthplace of Richard Conyers in 1725. After an education at Cambridge, Conyers was ordained in 1755 and became curate in the All Saints Church in the sprawling parish of Helmsley, North Yorkshire. He became rector there two years later and gained immediate popularity, even a reputation for great saintliness. Regular visitations, private conversations with any who appeared wayward and even the establishing of a time for corporate prayer for the young men of the parish were among the things that gave Richard Conyers such a reputation.

But one day Conyers read a verse in Scripture that frightened him: *Woe to you when all men speak well of you*. And all spoke well of Richard Conyers. Surely, he reasoned, he must be included in that dreadful 'Woe'. He fasted, he prayed, he made covenants with God, even signing them in his own blood. Nothing availed to ease his conscience. Perhaps he had been guilty of deceiving his parishioners as well as himself. At last on Christmas Day 1758 as he was walking slowly up the stairs in his home, burdened by a sense of his sins, another verse of Scripture flashed across his mind. *The blood of Jesus Christ his (God's) Son cleanses us from all sin.* Light dawned on his troubled mind. Surely this was the answer he had so urgently been seeking. 'I've found him, I've found him,' he cried in jubilation. 'I've found him whom my soul loves.' Clapping his hands with joy and relief he rushed up and down the stairs, and then backwards and forwards in his own room.

Unable to contain his excitement, he called together his friends to tell them what had happened. Word quickly spread and the next Sunday the church was packed. 'I have been in spiritual darkness until now,' he told his astonished congregation, 'and I have deceived you ...' Conyers then told them plainly of the only way to find acceptance with God—through the forgiveness of sin by the blood of the cross of Christ. Now all men did not speak well of him. But an amazing change took place in Helmsley as men and women responded to that same message of mercy and forgiveness. Neighbouring vicars were less impressed. How could they silence this man? At last they decided to report the strange events in Helmsley to the Archbishop of York, hoping he would 'defrock' him—strip him of his clerical gown.

Richard Conyers was summoned to preach before the Archbishop. Nor did he water down his message as he preached. 'Well, Conyers, you have given us a fine sermon,' the Archbishop snapped. 'Do I receive your Grace's approbation?' enquired Conyers. 'Approbation, approbation!' snorted the Archbishop. 'If you go on preaching such stuff you will drive all your parish mad.' But he did not defrock the Helmsley Rector, and Conyers continued to preach that same message of forgiveness of sins through Christ. These were the days that John Wesley and George Whitefield were preaching up and down the country and though Conyers did not join them in travelling around, he invited them to Helmsley whenever he heard they were in the area.

Conyers was greatly loved by the people of Helmsley and when their Rector accepted a call to minister in Deptford in 1767, they threatened to lie across the road to prevent his carriage from leaving. In the end he had to slip away at dead of night to avoid the anguish of parting. For the next twenty years Conyers had an effective London ministry, dying in 1787 at the age of sixty-two. His funeral sermon was preached by John Newton, the writer of the popular hymn:

> Amazing grace! how sweet the sound
> that saved a wretch like me.
> I once was lost, but now I'm found,
> was blind, but now I see.

21. Bishop Robert Ferrar: a Yorkshire martyr

It was a dark day for England when Mary I ascended the throne of England in 1553. Determined to reverse the progress of the Reformation of the English church which had been taking place, she set about a fearful regime of persecution in order to bring the land back under the domination of the Papacy and the Roman Catholic Church. This meant burning at the stake hundreds of noble Christian men and women who held religious convictions other than her own. And a Yorkshire man by the name of Robert Ferrar, was one of the first to suffer.

Born in Halifax in about 1506, he proceeded to Oxford in 1522 at the age of sixteen or seventeen—a critical period for the English church. For in 1526 William Tyndale's first translation of the New Testament into English was smuggled into the country from the Continent, hidden in bales of cloth. And Robert Ferrar was among a group of students who secretly studied the contraband. It was risky and life changing for the young man. The Bible was only readily available in Latin at the time and none but the clergy had access to it. Ferrar soon paid a price as Cardinal Wolsey rounded up anyone discovered reading these smuggled books, imprisoning many and destroying their books in a public bonfire.

During the years of Henry VIII's reign from 1509 to 1547 religious opinion see-sawed in line with the King's opinions: sometimes he burnt Protestants and at other times it would be Catholics. These were difficult years for those who had found new spiritual life and freedom through reading the Scriptures, but Ferrar trod carefully, becoming chaplain to the new Archbishop, Thomas Cranmer who served after the fall of Wolsey. Being a Yorkshire man Ferrar was sent to Nostell near Wakefield—the situation of a beautiful priory—to assist in the Dissolution of the Monasteries. He generally managed to stay out of trouble during this time.

When Henry died in 1547 his nine-year-old son Edward came to the throne and with the boy's love of the Scriptures and desire to promote the Reformation of the church, life became much easier for men like Robert Ferrar. These were perhaps his happiest years. With relaxed rules about the celibacy of the clergy, Robert married and enjoyed family life with Elizabeth and their three children.

He soon became chaplain to Edward Seymour, uncle of the young King, who virtually ruled the country while Edward was still a child. Ferrar was then sent to Wales to promote the Reformation of the church in that country and was made Bishop of St David's in Pembrokeshire. But problems soon arose. The Welsh resented the interference of an English man, let alone a Yorkshire man, in their affairs and were able to raise a lawsuit against Ferrar—a case he lost and as a result was subsequently imprisoned. Things became even worse when his patron Edward Seymour fell from power and was executed on trumped up charges.

Then came the unexpected death of young king Edward—not yet sixteen. It was a sorry day for England and for good men like Robert Ferrar. The writing was on the wall when Mary Tudor, elder daughter of Henry VIII, came to the throne in 1553, with the dogged purpose of stamping out the work of Reformation begun by her father and flowering under her young brother Edward. Targeting men like Ferrar, John Bradford, Thomas Cranmer, Nicholas Ridley and Hugh Latimer, her reign has gone down in history as one of unprecedented cruelty. Soon good and godly men and women were thrown into prison to await a prejudiced trial with the stake looming large on the horizon. The fearful toll of martyrdoms mounted. Almost three hundred men, women and young people were condemned to an agonising death at the stake.

Robert Ferrar's 'offence' of marrying paled into insignificance when his doctrinal beliefs were questioned, especially on issues such as the Mass. Ferrar denied the Catholic belief that the bread and wine of the Mass actually turned into the physical body and blood of Christ. No, he reasoned, these were only symbols of the body and blood of the Lord to remind his church of Christ's sacrifice for sin. This doctrine was anathema to Mary and to her bishops.

Trumped up charges were also laid at the door of this good man and though he denied them vehemently, he stood no chance against Bishop Stephen Gardiner and a prejudiced jury. Surely the best way to punish such a man was to send him for execution to a place where he was well known, reasoned Gardiner. Condemned to be burnt at the stake for his 'heresies', Ferrar was sent to Carmarthen in Wales, where he faced a fresh trial before the new Bishop of St David's—Henry Morgan. If he would agree to recant his faith and affirm the Catholic teachings on subjects such as the authority of the Church against that of the Bible and the doctrines of the Mass, he might live. If not, he must die. Robert Ferrar stood firm.

As 30th March 1555 dawned men were busy tying up piles of faggots around a central stake not far from the market cross in Carmarthen. Asked by a friend if he could face the fire without flinching, Ferrar said—perhaps somewhat unwisely—that if he stirred one muscle in the flames, then his friend could disbelieve all the truths for which Ferrar was prepared to die. Chained to the stake this brave man kept his word and stood without moving as the flames licked around him—until one bystander in mercy ended Ferrar's suffering by striking him on the head. So died a noble Christian man *of whom the world was not worthy.*[7]

---

[7] Hebrews 11:38.

Time would fail me to tell of ...

So said the writer of the Epistle to the Hebrews in his famous eleventh chapter as he described the deeds of the men and women of faith from the past. Having told of Abel, Abraham, Jacob, Moses and others, he exclaims as if in despair that he could mention many more *of whom the world was not worthy*. But time was at a premium and he could only refer briefly to others who had displayed astonishing faith and surmounted mountainous difficulties in their devotion to God. Although not in the same category, it is amazing how many truly remarkable people were born or served in this one fine county of Great Britain—Yorkshire. And these few short descriptions may be added to those already written about in these pages. Undoubtedly there are countless others who could well have found a place in this record.

Benjamin Waugh

Born in 1839 in Settle, on the verge of the Yorkshire Dales, eight-year-old Benjamin Waugh had just lost his tender-hearted mother, but from her he had already seen an example of Christian love and compassion towards the suffering of others. In an age of great cruelty and injustice, young Benjamin early exhibited that same spirit. When two young boys were hauled up to court for stealing a turnip to make into a lantern, an incident meriting a possible beating but not imprisonment, Benjamin, still only a teenager himself, appealed for them in court, saying he had done the same thing but was never found out. Marrying and entering the ministry of the church in 1865 at the age of twenty-six, Waugh eventually moved to East Greenwich in London. Here he witnessed appalling cruelty to children. The sexual exploitation of young girls or jail sentences for boys stealing a loaf of bread often to feed younger siblings, distressed him. Even animals were treated with greater kindness. Something must be done. Campaigning tirelessly, he at last managed to establish the National Society for the Prevention of Cruelty to Children (NSPCC) in 1884—an organisation that has done countless good for needy and vulnerable children over its more than one hundred and thirty years of existence. Waugh's death in 1908 has left the world a poorer place, but his legacy lives on.

George Perfect

George Perfect is largely remembered for writing the moving and memorable hymn: 'Jesus was slain for me at Calvary'. The words sum up the priorities and beliefs of this fine Yorkshire man, born in Bingley on 3 January 1882. It also explains his motivation in going to Lagos in Nigeria in 1932 to start an evangelistic work in that part of the world, a ministry that would extend to Ghana— bringing many thousands to faith in Jesus Christ. When he was dying in 1958, Perfect's last request was for someone to bring him his New Testament, now battered and worn. It had been his comfort in life and then also in death. His hymn lives on as George Perfect still teaches Christian congregations to sing:

> Pardoned is all my sin,
> at Calvary,
> cleansed is my heart within,
> at Calvary.
> Now robes of praise I wear,
> gone are my grief and care,

Christ bore my burdens there,
at Calvary.

John Henry Jowett

When Josiah and Hannah Jowett's baby, John Henry, was born in Halifax in 1863 they would have been astonished had they known the future that lay before their son. Their highest ambition for their infant appears to have been that he should become a lawyer's clerk. But God had other purposes for John Henry. His Sunday School teacher turned the lad's thoughts to God and as he grew older John's heart's wish was to become a preacher of that gospel that had transformed his young life.

After theological training J. H. Jowett became pastor of St James' Congregational Church in Newcastle. His winsome preaching style and evangelistic zeal were deeply effective and before long the congregation had almost trebled from six hundred to fifteen hundred. But it also drew the attention of no less a figure than R. W. Dale of Carrs Lane Congregational Church in Birmingham who was approaching the end of his ministry. On several occasions Jowett was invited to preach at Carrs Lane. So acceptable was he to that burgeoning congregation that when Dale died in 1895 Carrs Lane warmly invited Jowett to follow him as their pastor. From 1896 until 1911 Jowett's clear preaching rang out in Birmingham transforming many lives from dissipation to godliness.

But there were rival churches who were after such preaching. After visiting a Presbyterian church in New York that American congregation persisted in its invitations to Jowett to come to its pulpit. At last after refusing two urgent requests, a third was sent and Jowett felt that this was God's purpose for his life. For the next six years he served that New York congregation. One final period of ministry remained; after Dr Campbell Morgan's period of retirement from his ministry in the magnificent Westminster Chapel pulpit in London, he was on the look-out for a good preacher. And Campbell Morgan knew one when he heard one. In 1917 he recommended that J. H. Jowett should be invited to follow him. Six years at Westminster left Jowett a tired man with declining health. In 1923, just a year after retiring, John Henry Jowett died at the age of sixty.

James Berry

Other well-respected and influential preachers and evangelists born in Yorkshire include Herbert Silverwood and Leonard Ravenhill but the most colourful of all must surely be James Berry, one-time public hangman. The grim expression resting on Berry's face shown in surviving pictures suggests a man well-suited to his ghastly vocation but one he chose out of desperate need to save his family from starvation. Berry was born in Heckmondwike, not far from Dewsbury in 1852, the thirteenth child of fourteen in the family. With little aptitude for book learning, he joined the police force, but finding himself in need after eight years applied for the now vacant post of public executioner.

Despite his unsavoury task, Berry was in fact a deeply sensitive man, finding it difficult to eat or drink in the days leading up to an execution. To his credit he sought means to make this end-of-life ordeal less horrific by scientifically working out the length of drop needed to correspond more accurately to the criminal's weight so that the end would come with greater speed. In all he was responsible for one hundred and thirty-one executions during his eight years of employment, charging ten guineas for each grizzly transaction with board and lodging at the prison before the final day. He even wrote a book entitled 'My Experiences as an Executioner', with accounts of a number of the deaths of the condemned men and women he had supervised. But the emotional price was high. In the end James Berry suffered serious depression and had every intention of taking his own life.

Then God intervened. As Berry planned to leap from a moving train a young Christian with an ardent wish to see men and women turned to Christ for salvation spoke to him. Earnestly begging Berry to accompany him to an evangelistic meeting, he had the joy of seeing the unhappy man transformed by the grace of God. We read 'Mr Berry fully surrendered himself, accepted God's precious gift and was at once filled with rest and joy, praising God.' He resigned his job and for the remainder of James Berry's unusual life he travelled the country working as an evangelist and also repudiating the death penalty. He died in 1913 at the age of sixty-one. The death penalty was not abolished in Britain until 1964.

Smith Wigglesworth

When Smith Wigglesworth was born in 1859 to an impoverished family in Menston, in the borough of Bradford, his family may well have despaired of raising the boy. In fact, he lived to the grand age of eighty-eight. But the early years were bleak. The boy started manual work at the age of six, drifting from one job to another. He did not learn to read until after his marriage. But significantly God worked in the child's life at an early age. He began to pray that he might know God as he pulled turnips in the field. And it was a prayer God answered. As he was attending a Methodist church, the words of a hymn spoke clearly to him of the Lamb of God who could cleanse him from his sins. With childlike faith young Smith Wigglesworth believed and a life of amazing usefulness in God's kingdom began—his own mother was the first to whom he spoke and her life too was changed.

With a passion for the needy and uneducated, Smith's first significant work was among young people, first in Liverpool and then back in Bradford. He believed genuinely and deeply in the power of prayer and witnessed amazing miracles in answer to his urgent cries to God. But when he linked up with the growing Pentecostal movement, together with his wife Polly, his urgent gospel preaching was used to bring thousands into the kingdom of God. We may not agree with some of the emphases of his ministry but undoubtedly this man belongs in the ranks of great Yorkshire men used by God.

John Harrison, William Bradford and Thomas Langton

Among others whose contribution we could highlight we may mention John Harrison, born near Wakefield in 1693, a genius clockmaker who invented a clock that could accurately measure the longitude position of ships while at sea, a problem that had mystified even Sir Isaac Newton. By this invention the lives of many sailors were saved. William Bradford, born in Austerfield near Doncaster in 1589, was among the early Separatists who sailed to New England on the *Mayflower* in 1620 in search of religious freedom. He was five times Governor of Massachusetts. And lastly we cannot omit Thomas Langton of Malton, whose ceaseless travels and warm evangelistic zeal earned him the title of The Yorkshire Evangelist

Without question the county of Yorkshire has produced some of the greatest men and women that our land has ever known. There is something fierce, strong-minded, inventive and doggedly determined about the Yorkshire temperament that defies description, but explains its greatness, particularly when motivated by the glory of God. We have not included present day Yorkshire characters for obvious reasons, but suffice it to say there are a number who well deserve a place in such a record, including our own indomitable evangelist Roger Carswell—a born and bred Yorkshire man.

Some of these men and women whose lives are recorded in these pages had outstanding gifts and would find a natural place in the annals of secular history for their astonishing achievements and contribution to the welfare of the human race. We need only mention John Wycliffe, William Wilberforce and Samuel Marsden as examples of those falling into this category. Others, however, would never receive a reference in the history books— men and women largely forgotten. One thing marks them out, however: their spiritual achievement through the power of the God of glory. Perhaps they had little natural gift: John Oxtoby and Ruth Clark might be suggested as examples of those who fall into this category. Yet through the grace of God and their unwavering faith in the Lord Jesus Christ they outstrip many whom this world reveres and honours.

Certainly Yorkshire has given birth to an exceptional amount of natural gift and achievement, but the purpose of this slim book is to demonstrate what God may do through any man or woman who casts himself on the Lord Jesus Christ in faith for forgiveness of sin and mercy through the sacrifice of the cross. Like the boy in the gospel record who offered to Christ his five loaves and two fish, modest natural gifts may be multiplied a thousandfold for the blessing of others in God's purposes. Lives dedicated to God's glory can have astonishing and unforeseen consequences in this world and as a bonus a hope of heaven and an abundance of joy in a world to come. Surely such should be the ambition of every man and woman whether from Yorkshire or indeed from the furthest reaches of this earthly sphere.

...and a postscript from Roger Carswell

Whether you live in Wetwang, Blubberhouses, Idle, Swillington or the Land of Nod[8] or other parts of Yorkshire, or for that matter anywhere else (even Lancashire!), the greatest need of each individual is to make sure that he or she is right with God. Jesus said that he came into the world to save sinners. And we all qualify!

They may not put a statue in the park to commemorate our lives when eventually we die, we may not even fill the obituary columns of our local newspaper, but each person matters, and the most crucial issue for everyone is whether we have come to know God in a personal and eternal way.

The Bible teaches that forgiveness is not earned, and heaven is not a reward. They are gifts, purchased by Jesus in his dying and rising again, and offered to us. He who loved us is willing to make us his sons and daughters. Hell is for those who refuse God's offer of salvation; heaven is for those who turn from their own ways to trust him as Lord and Saviour.

Anne Brontë wrote words, which you could pray and make your own:

> My God! Oh let me call Thee mine!
> Weak, wretched sinner though I be,
> my trembling heart would fain be Thine,
> my feeble faith still clings to Thee.

---

8 A real place

Not only for the past I grieve,
the future fills me with dismay;
unless Thou hasten to relieve,
I know my heart will fall away.

I cannot say my faith is strong,
I dare not hope my love is great,
but strength and love to Thee belong,
Oh do not leave me desolate!

I know I owe my all to Thee.
Oh! take my heart I cannot give.
Do Thou my Strength, my Saviour be:
 and make me to Thy glory live!

The Bible says: *Whoever calls on the name of the Lord shall be saved.*[9]

And the Bible makes it clear that heaven is far better than even Yorkshire!

---

[9] Romans 10:13